The Observer's Pocket Series

AIRCRAFT

The Observer Books

A POCKET REFERENCE SERIES
COVERING NATURAL HISTORY, TRANSPORT, THE ARTS ETC

The Observer's Book of
AIRCRAFT

COMPILED BY
WILLIAM GREEN

WITH SILHOUETTES BY
DENNIS PUNNETT

DESCRIBING 158 AIRCRAFT
WITH 278 ILLUSTRATIONS

1972 Edition

FREDERICK WARNE & CO LTD
FREDERICK WARNE & CO INC
LONDON · NEW YORK

© FREDERICK WARNE & CO LTD
LONDON, ENGLAND

1972

Twenty-first Edition 1972

Recommended by
THE AIR SCOUTS' DEPARTMENT
of
THE SCOUTS' ASSOCIATION

LIBRARY OF CONGRESS CATALOG CARD NO: 57–4425

ISBN 0 7232 1507 3

Printed in Great Britain

INTRODUCTION TO THE 1972 EDITION

With this, the 21st annual edition, the *Observer's Book of Aircraft* comes of age. The basic format has remained essentially unchanged over the past score-and-one years; the three-view general arrangement silhouettes are prepared by the same draughtsman, and the number of pages has remained unchanged, as has the number of aircraft illustrated and described. Indeed, the only obvious changes over the intervening years have been the retail price and the use of metric in addition to Imperial measures. But a comparison of the aircraft included in this edition and that of 1952 reveals clearly the enormity of the changes that have taken place over this period in the shape, size and performance of both civil and military aeroplanes.

It is perhaps instructive to note that almost exactly one-third of the aircraft types included in the 1952 edition of the *Observer's Book of Aircraft* are still to be seen in the world's skies, and one cannot but help wonder as to what proportion of those included in the pages that follow will enjoy such longevity. At the time the 1952 edition was prepared, the only turbojet-driven commercial transport extant was the de Havilland Comet, and the Korean conflict had entered its final year, with encounters between F-86 Sabre fighters of the USAF and Soviet-supplied North Korean MiG-15s virtually a daily occurrence. As these words are penned, few indeed are the commercial passenger services that are *not* flown by turbojet-driven airliners, but the Sabre is still firing its guns in anger, its pilots now being members of the Pakistan Air Force and its primary targets still being progeny of the Mikoyan-Gurevich design bureau, but this time MiG-21s flown by the Indian Air Force.

Apart from the changes in appearance and performance of the aircraft types represented, there has been one other change over the years: the ratio of civil to military aircraft types has increased in the content matter of the *Observer's Book of Aircraft*. The former do not yet preponderate, however, and their increased numbers merely reflect the growth of civil aviation rather than a tendency towards a more peaceful world. In fact, only four of 1971's aircraft débutantes were intended specifically for civil application, while but one of those scheduled to commence their flight test programmes this year, the Airbus A-300B, is a commercial aeroplane, underlining the fact that emphasis remains on the development of military aircraft.

Insufficient information had become available at the time of closing for press to permit inclusion of the most recent Soviet combat aircraft, such as the variable-geometry air superiority fighter and strategic bomber, dubbed *Fearless* and *Backfire* respectively by NATO, but western military débutantes that appear for the first time in this edition include the Lockheed S-3A Viking ASW aircraft, the Northrop YA-9A and Fairchild YA-10A attack aircraft, and the McDonnell Douglas F-15 fighter.

WILLIAM GREEN

AERITALIA-AERMACCHI AM-3C

Country of Origin: Italy.
Type: Battlefield surveillance and forward air control aircraft.
Power Plant: One 340 hp Piaggio-built Lycoming GSO-480-B1B6 six-cylinder horizontally-opposed engine.
Performance: (At normal loaded weight) Max. speed, 161 mph (260 km/h) at sea level, 173 mph (278 km/h) at 8,000 ft (2 440 m); initial climb, 1,378 ft/min (7 m/sec); service ceiling, 27,560 ft (8 400 m); max. range with 30 min reserves, 615 mls (990 km).
Weights: Empty equipped, 2,548 lb (1 156 kg); normal loaded, 3,307 lb (1 500 kg); max., 3,858 lb (1 750 kg).
Armament: Two underwing stores stations each stressed for loads up to 375 lb (170 kg), external armament including two pods each containing a pair of 7,62-mm guns with 1,000 rpg, or two Matra 125 packs each of six 2·75-in rockets.
Status: First of two flying prototypes flown May 12, 1967, followed by second on August 22, 1968. Both initially fitted with Continental GTSIO-520-C engine (see 1968 edition) but re-engined with GSO-480-B1B6 as AM-3C in 1969. Production deliveries against export order for 40 aircraft for South African Army to commence 1972.
Notes: AM-3C evaluated during 1970–71 by Italian Army and Air Force in competition with SIAI-Marchetti SM.1019 (see page 210), and licence manufacture to be undertaken in South Africa by the Armaments Development and Production Corporation.

AERITALIA-AERMACCHI AM-3C

Dimensions: Span, 41 ft 5⅓ in (12,64 m); length, 29 ft 5½ in (8,98 m); height, 8 ft 11 in (2,72 m); wing area, 219·15 sq ft (20,36 m²).

AERITALIA (FIAT) G.91Y

Country of Origin: Italy.

Type: Single-seat light tactical fighter-bomber and reconnaissance aircraft.

Power Plant: Two 2,725 lb (1 236 kg) dry and 4,080 lb (1 850 kg) reheat General Electric J85-GE-13A turbojets.

Performance: Max. speed, 690 mph (1 110 km/h) or Mach 0·9 at sea level, 670 mph (1 080 km/h) or Mach 0·95 at 32,810 ft (10 000 m); range cruise at 490 ft (150 m), 390 mph (630 km/h); typical tactical radius for lo-lo-lo mission with 2,910-lb (1 320-kg) payload, 240 mls (385 km); ferry range with two 176 Imp gal (800 l) auxiliary tanks and 10% reserves, 2,110 mls (3 400 km); max. initial climb, 17,000 ft/min (86,36 m/sec); service ceiling, 41,000 ft (12 500 m).

Weights: Empty, 8,598 lb (3 900 kg); normal max. take-off, 17,196 lb (7 800 kg); max. overload take-off, 19,180 lb (8 700 kg).

Armament: Two 30-mm DEFA 552 cannon. Four underwing stores stations for max. of 4,000 lb (1 814 kg) ordnance.

Status: First of two prototypes flown December 27, 1966, and first of 20 pre-production aircraft flown July 1968. Delivery of 55 production aircraft to Italian Air Force scheduled for completion during 1972.

Notes: Prototype of a modified version with more advanced avionics (including Saab bombing computer) for evaluation by Switzerland was flown on October 16, 1970. This, the G.91YS, features two additional underwing stores points each able to carry a Sidewinder AAM. The G.91YT is a projected two-seat training version.

8

AERITALIA (FIAT) G.91Y

Dimensions: Span, 29 ft $6\frac{1}{2}$ in (9,01 m); length, 38 ft $3\frac{1}{2}$ in (11,67 m); height, 14 ft $6\frac{1}{3}$ in (4,43 m); wing area, 195·149 sq ft (18,13 m²).

AERITALIA (FIAT) G.222

Country of Origin: Italy.

Type: General-purpose military transport.

Power Plant: Two 2,970 shp General Electric CT64-820 turboprops. (Proposed) Two 3,400 shp T64-P4D turboprops.

Performance: (Estimated with T64-P4D engines) Max. speed, 329 mph (530 km/h) at sea level; normal cruise, 273 mph (440 km/h) at 14,750 ft (4 500 m); range with 11,025-lb (5 000-kg) payload, 1,920 mls (3 250 km), with max. fuel, 3,262 mls (5 250 km); max. initial climb rate, 1,890 ft/min (9,6 m/sec).

Weights: Empty, 29,320 lb (13 300 kg); empty equipped, 32,408 lb (14 700 kg); max. take-off, 57,320 lb (26 000 kg).

Accommodation: Flight crew of three or four and seats for 44 fully-equipped troops or 40 paratroops. Alternative loads include 36 casualty stretchers, two jeep-type vehicles or equivalent freight.

Status: First of two prototypes flown July 18, 1970, followed by second prototype on July 22, 1971. An order for 40 aircraft for the Italian Air Force was confirmed at the beginning of 1972, and it is anticipated that deliveries of the G.222 will be made 1973–74.

Notes: Prototypes powered by CT64-820 turboprops and unpressurised, but the proposed production model will have uprated T64-P4D turboprops and provision for pressurisation. The G.222 is intended as a successor to some of the Italian Air Force's ageing Fairchild C-119 transports.

10

AERITALIA (FIAT) G.222

Dimensions: Span, 94 ft 5¾ in (28,80 m); length, 74 ft 5½ in (22,70 m); height, 32 ft 1¾ in (9,80 m); wing area, 970·9 sq ft (90,2 m²).

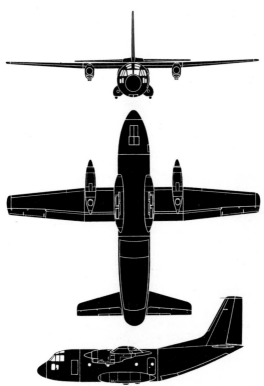

AERMACCHI M.B.326K

Country of Origin: Italy.

Type: Single-seat operational trainer and close-support aircraft.

Power Plant: One 4,000 lb (1 814 kg) Rolls-Royce Viper 632-43 turbojet.

Performance: (Estimated) Max. speed without external stores, 550 mph (885 km/h) at 19,685 ft (6 000 m); max. cruise, 497 mph (800 km/h); ferry range with two 90 Imp. gal. (409 l) underwing auxiliary tanks, 1,400 mls (2 250 km).

Weights: Empty equipped, 6,298 lb (2 857 kg); loaded (clean), 9,678 lb (4 390 kg); max., 12,000 lb (5 443 kg).

Armament: Two 30-mm DEFA or Aden cannon with 150 rpg. Six underwing stores stations of which four stressed for loads up to 1,000 lb (453,5 kg) and two for loads up to 750 lb (340 kg). Max. external ordnance load of 4,500 lb (2 040 kg).

Status: First prototype M.B.326K flown August 22, 1970 with Viper 540 turbojet and second prototype with Viper 632 flown May 1971. Flight test programme scheduled for completion early 1972 with production commencing during the course of the year.

Notes: M.B.326K is a single-seat dual-purpose derivative of the two-seat M.B.326G with the 3,410 lb (1 547 kg) Viper 540 turbojet (see 1970 edition). Apart from a more powerful turbojet, built-in cannon armament and a single-seat cockpit, the M.B.326K embodies some local strengthening of the forward fuselage structure, a high-flotation undercarriage, and provision for armour protection. Licence production in South Africa by Armament Development and Production Corporation is anticipated.

12

AERMACCHI M.B.326K

Dimensions: Span (over tip tanks), 35 ft 6¾ in (10,84 m); length, 34 ft 10⅞ in (10,64 m); height, 12 ft 1¾ in (3,70 m); wing area, 207·958 sq ft (19,32 m²).

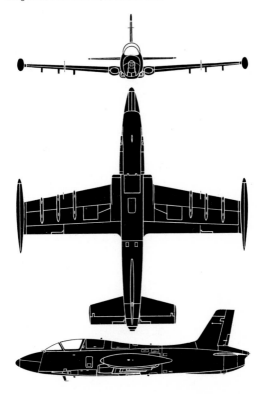

AERO L 39

Country of Origin: Czechoslovakia.

Type: Tandem two-seat basic and advanced trainer.

Power Plant: One 3,307 lb (1 500 kg) Walter Titan (Ivchenko AI-25V) turbofan.

Performance: Max. speed, 379 mph (610 km/h) at sea level, 454 mph (730 km/h) at 16,400 ft (5 000 m); range on internal fuel with 5% reserves, 680 mls (1 100 km), with tip-tanks and no reserves, 930 mls (1 500 km); initial climb, 3,740 ft/min (19 m/sec).

Weights: Empty, 6,283 lb (2 850 kg); normal loaded, 8,377 lb (3 800 kg); max. take-off, 9,480 lb (4 300 kg).

Status: First of five flying prototypes flown on November 4, 1968, and first of pre-production batch of 10 aircraft joined test programme during 1971 with full production commencing in 1972. Orders for 700 L 39s had been placed by beginning of 1971, including 300 for the Soviet Union. Czechoslovak Air Force expected to receive up to 300 during 1972–75.

Notes: The L 39 is intended as a successor for the L 29 Delfin, and a 3,968-lb (1 800-kg) version of the Titan (AI-25VM) with a two-stage fan is under development for the production model. An afterburning Titan of some 4,410 lb (2 000 kg) is being developed for a light strike version of the L 39. This model will feature wing hard points for gun pods, ASMs and bombs, and is intended primarily for sale in Africa and Asia.

14

AERO L 39

Dimensions: Span, 29 ft $10\frac{3}{4}$ in (9,11 m); length, 39 ft $10\frac{2}{3}$ in (12,12 m); height, 14 ft $4\frac{1}{4}$ in (4,38 m); wing area, 202·4 sq ft (18,8 m²).

AÉROSPATIALE SE 210 CARAVELLE 12

Country of Origin: France.

Type: Short- to medium-range commercial transport.

Power Plant: Two 14,500 lb (6 577 kg) Pratt & Whitney JT8D-9 turbofans.

Performance: Max. cruise at 25,000 ft (7 620 m), 504 mph (812 km/h) at 110,230 lb (50 000 kg); range with max. fuel at 32,000 ft (9 750 m), 2,423 mls (3 900 km) with 20,170 lb (9 150 kg) payload; range with max. payload (29,100 lb/13 200 kg), 1,693 mls (2 725 km).

Weights: Empty, 65,050 lb (29 500 kg); basic operational, 70,100 lb (31 800 kg); max., 123,460 lb (56 000 kg).

Accommodation: Normal flight crew of four and five-abreast seating for 118–128 tourist-class passengers, or mixed-class layout for 16 (four-abreast) first-class and 88 tourist-class passengers.

Status: Certificated early in 1971, the Caravelle 12 is the latest progressive development of the basic SE 210 airliner, and the first example of this lengthened model was flown for the first time on October 29, 1970. Seven Caravelle 12s have been ordered by the Danish independent operator Sterling Airways which has a further four Caravelles of this type on option, the first example being delivered to Sterling on March 12, 1971. Five Caravelle 12s are to be leased by Air Inter.

Notes: Caravelle 12 is a long-body version of the Caravelle Super B (see 1966 edition) with an additional 6 ft 6¾ in (2,00 m) fuselage section inserted ahead of the wing and a 3 ft 11½ in (1,21 m) section aft, plus local structural strengthening.

AÉROSPATIALE SE 210 CARAVELLE 12

Dimensions: Span, 112 ft 6½ in (34,30 m); length, 118 ft 10½ in (36,24 m); height, 29 ft 7 in (9,01 m); wing area, 1,579 sq ft (146,7 m²).

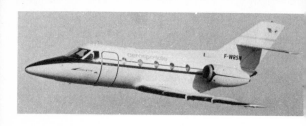

AÉROSPATIALE SN 600 CORVETTE

Country of Origin: France.

Type: Light business executive transport.

Power Plant: Two 2,310 lb (1 048 kg) Pratt & Whitney JT15D-4 turbofans.

Performance: (Estimated) Max. cruise, 466 mph (750 km/h) at 25,000 ft (7 620 m); econ. cruise, 391 mph (630 km/h) at 36,090 ft (11 000 m); range with 12 passengers and 45 min reserves, 1,100 mls (1 770 km); max. range with auxiliary fuel and 45 min reserves, 1,560 mls (2 510 km); initial climb, 3,000 ft/min (15,25 m/sec).

Weights: Empty equipped, 7,698 lb (3 492 kg); max. take-off, 13,448 lb (6 100 kg).

Accommodation: Crew of one or two on flight deck and normal seating for 6–12 passengers in individual seats.

Status: Prototype flown on July 16, 1970, and first of two pre-production examples scheduled to fly at the end of 1972 with the second in March 1973. First two production aircraft to join test programme during 1973 with initial deliveries in 1974.

Notes: First prototype destroyed on March 23, 1971, this aircraft being illustrated above. Second prototype (illustrated on opposite page) features redesigned and lengthened rear fuselage, and will be flown with 2,205 lb (1 000 kg) JT15D-1 turbofans. The third will fly with JT15D-4s, and in the autumn of 1974 a Corvette will be flown with 2,755 lb (1 250 kg) SNECMA-Turboméca Larzac turbofans which are to be offered as alternative power plants to the JT15D-4s. The Corvette is competing with the Falcon 10 (see pages 72–73) for an *Armée de l'Air* order.

AÉROSPATIALE SN 600 CORVETTE

Dimensions: Span, 41 ft 11⅞ in (12,80 m); length, 45 ft 8½ in (13,93 m); height, 14 ft 3⅔ in (4,36 m); wing area, 236·8 sq ft (22,0 m²).

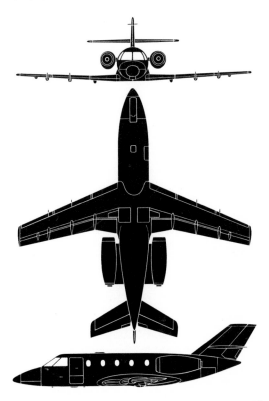

AÉROSPATIALE N 262C FRÉGATE

Country of Origin: France.

Type: Light short-range feederliner.

Power Plant: Two 1,360 shp Turboméca Bastan VIIA turboprops.

Performance: Max. speed, 260 mph (418 km/h); max. cruise, 254 mph (408 km/h) at 15,090 ft (4 600 m); normal cruise, 247 mph (397 km/h); range with max. fuel and no reserves, 1,490 mls (2 400 km), with max. payload and no reserves, 650 mls (1 050 km); initial climb, 1,496 ft/min (7,6 m/sec); service ceiling, 26,250 ft (8 000 m).

Weights: Empty equipped, 15,286 lb (6 934 kg); basic operational, 15,873 lb (7 200 kg); max. take-off, 23,370 lb (10 600 kg).

Accommodation: Basic flight crew of two and standard seating for 26 passengers in three-abreast rows (two to starboard and one to port of aisle). Alternative arrangement for 29 passengers.

Status: Development aircraft for C-series of the Frégate flown in July 1968 and series production of N 262C initiated 1970 alongside military counterpart, the N 262D for the *Armée de l'Air*.

Notes: The N 262C is similar to the initial production model of the Frégate, the N 262A, apart from its more powerful engines (the earlier model having Bastan VIs) and new wing-tips improving low-speed handling. The *Armée de l'Air* has accepted six A-series Frégates and, from August 1971, was in process of receiving 18 D-series aircraft, and the *Aéro-navale* had previously received 15 examples of the N 262A model.

AÉROSPATIALE N 262C FRÉGATE

Dimensions: Span, 71 ft 10$\frac{1}{4}$ in (21,90 m); length, 63 ft 3 in (19,28 m); height, 20 ft 4 in (6,21 m); wing area, 592 sq ft (55,0 m²).

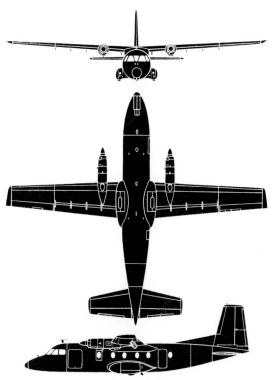

AÉROSPATIALE ST-10 DIPLOMATE

Country of Origin: France.

Type: Light cabin monoplane.

Power Plant: One 200 hp Lycoming IO-360-C1B four-cylinder horizontally-opposed engine.

Performance: Max. speed, 186 mph (300 km/h) at sea level; cruise at 75% power, 168 mph (270 km/h); range with four passengers, 860 mls (1 385 km); initial climb, 1,005 ft/min (5,1 m/sec); service ceiling, 16,400 ft (5 000 m).

Weights: Empty equipped, 1,594 lb (723 kg); max. take-off, 2,690 lb (1 220 kg).

Accommodation: Pilot and three passengers in side-by-side pairs.

Status: First prototype flown November 7, 1967. Extensive modifications introduced prior to certification programme, type approval being received on November 26, 1969, with production deliveries commencing early in 1970.

Notes: The Diplomate employs a number of components common to the four-seat GY-80 Horizon which it supplants in the Aérospatiale range of light cabin monoplanes. Dual controls and full blind-flying instrumentation are standard and the Diplomate is claimed to be particularly suitable for airline pilot IFR navigation training, and has been adopted for this task by Varig of Brazil which has taken delivery of six aircraft of this type.

AÉROSPATIALE ST-10 DIPLOMATE

Dimensions: Span, 31 ft $9\frac{3}{4}$ in (9,70 m); length, 23 ft $9\frac{7}{8}$ in (7,26 m); height, 9 ft $5\frac{1}{2}$ in (2,88 m); wing area, 139·93 sq ft (13 m²).

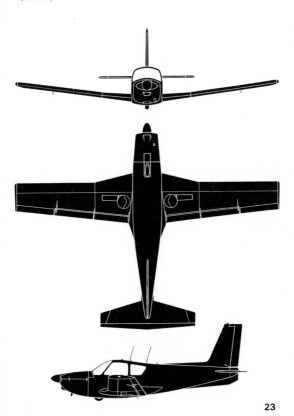

AÉROSPATIALE MS 894A
RALLYE MINERVA 220

Country of Origin: France.
Type: Light cabin monoplane.
Power Plant: One 220 hp Franklin 6A-350-C1 six-cylinder horizontally-opposed engine.
Performance: Max. speed, 165 mph (266 km/h) at sea level; cruise at 75% power, 155 mph (249 km/h) at 4,920 ft (1 500 m); range with max. fuel, 994 mls (1 600 km); initial climb, 984 ft/min (5,0 m/sec); service ceiling, 16,400 ft (5 000 m).
Weights: Empty equipped, 1,355 lb (615 kg); max. take-off, 2,425 lb (1 100 kg).
Accommodation: Two individual seats in front and bench seat for two persons at rear.
Status: The Minerva 220 is one of the current production versions of the basic Rallye design which has been manufactured in progressively refined versions since 1960, and flew for the first time on May 12, 1967, deliveries commencing in 1968. It is marketed in the USA by Aerocon-BFA which has contracted to take 100 in 1972.
Notes: An improved version of the Rallye Commodore, the first four-seat version of the basic Rallye design. Externally similar, the Rallye Commodore is available in two versions, the MS 892 Rallye Commodore 150 with a 150 hp Lycoming O-320-E2A and the MS 893 Rallye Commodore 180 with a 180 hp Lycoming O-360-A2A. The MS 894C (illustrated above) is a version of the Minerva 220 with a wheel-ski undercarriage.

AÉROSPATIALE MS 894A RALLYE MINERVA 220

Dimensions: Span, 31 ft 6¼ in (9,61 m); length, 23 ft 5¾ in (7,16 m); height, 9 ft 2¼ in (2,80 m); wing area, 132 sq ft (12,30 m²).

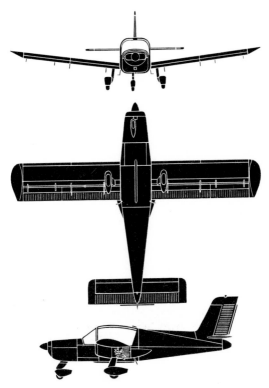

AIRBUS A-300B1

Country of Origin: International consortium.
Type: Short- to medium-range commercial transport.
Power Plant: Two 49,000 lb (22 226 kg) General Electric CF6-50A turbofans.
Performance: (Estimated) Max. cruise, 582 mph (937 km/h) at 25,000 ft (7 620 m); range with max. payload and reserves for 230-mile (370-km) diversion and 45 min hold at 5,000 ft (1 525 m), 1,290 mls (2 070 km), with max. fuel and same reserves, 2,425 mls (3 900 km).
Weights: (Estimated) Operational empty, 176,430 lb (80 030 kg); max. take-off, 291,000 lb (132 000 kg).
Accommodation: Basic flight crew of three, and various arrangements for 200–300 passengers in six-, seven-, or eight-abreast seating. Typical arrangement provides for 259 passengers in eight-abreast seating with two aisles.
Status: Seven aircraft, including one static test specimen, being built for flight test and certification, with first aircraft to fly October–November 1972. Certification planned for November–December 1973.
Notes: The A-300 is being manufactured by an international consortium comprising Aérospatiale (France), Deutsche Airbus (Federal Germany), Hawker Siddeley Aviation (UK), CASA (Spain), and Fokker-VFW (Netherlands), the programme being managed by Airbus Industrie. Air France has ordered the A-300B2 with three more rows of seats than the basic B1 described above. Projected derivatives include the A-300B3 with 51,000 lb (23 130 kg) CF6-50C turbofans and a 2,650-mile (4 260-km) range, and the A-300B7 with a stretched fuselage accommodating up to 325 passengers.

AIRBUS A-300B1

Dimensions: Span, 147 ft 1¼ in (44,84 m); length, 167 ft 2¼ in (50,96 m); height, 54 ft 4 in (16,56 m); wing area, 2,799 sq ft (260,0 m²).

AMERICAN AVIATION AA-1A TRAINER

Country of Origin: USA.
Type: Light training and utility aircraft.
Power Plant: One 108 hp Lycoming O-235-C2C four-cylinder horizontally-opposed engine.
Performance: Max. speed, 138 mph (222 km/h) at sea level; max. cruise (75% power), 125 mph (201 km/h) between 3,500 ft (1 070 m) and 8,000 ft (2 440 m); econ. cruise, 112 mph (180 km/h) at 10,000 ft (3 050 m); range at econ. cruise, 500 mls (804 km); initial climb, 760 ft/min (3,86 m/sec); service ceiling, 13,750 ft (4 190 m).
Weights: Empty equipped, 966 lb (438 kg); max. take-off, 1,500 lb (680 kg).
Accommodation: Two individual seats side-by-side with dual controls.
Status: Prototype of AA-1A flown on March 25, 1970, and first production example flown on November 6, 1970 with deliveries commencing January 14, 1971.
Notes: The AA-1A is a specialised training version of the AA-1 Yankee light cabin monoplane (see 1969 edition), which, in turn, was derived from the Bede BD-1. The AA-1A differs from the AA-1 primarily in having a redesigned aerofoil producing a higher lift coefficient and dual controls as standard. Both the AA-1 Yankee and AA-1A Trainer were being manufactured in parallel at the beginning of 1972.

AMERICAN AVIATION AA-1A TRAINER

Dimensions: Span, 24 ft 6 in (7,47 m); length, 19 ft 2½ in
(5,85 m); height, 6 ft 9½ in (2,07 m); wing area, 100·92 sq ft
(9,38 m²).

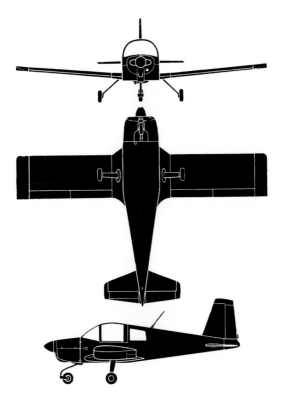

AMERICAN AVIATION AA-5 TRAVELER

Country of Origin: USA.
Type: Light cabin monoplane.
Power Plant: One 150 hp Lycoming O-320-E2G four-cylinder horizontally-opposed engine.
Performance: Max. speed, 151 mph (243 km/h) at sea level; cruise at 75% power, 141 mph (227 km/h) at 8,000 ft (2 440 m); range with max. fuel, 625 mls (1 006 km); initial climb, 690 ft/min (3,5 m/sec).
Weights: Empty equipped, 1,180 lb (535 kg); max. take-off, 2,150 lb (975 kg).
Accommodation: Pilot and three passengers in pairs in four separate seats.
Status: The prototype AA-5 Traveler was first flown on August 21, 1970, production deliveries following on certification in December 1971.
Notes: The AA-5 Traveler is essentially an enlarged version of the two-seat AA-1 Yankee with which it possesses considerable structural commonality. Production of the Traveler has been given precedence over that of an earlier American Aviation four-seater, the AA-2 Patriot which embodies major design changes and demands substantial new tooling. The AA-2 commenced its flight test programme in 1970, and development was continuing at the beginning of 1972.

30

AMERICAN AVIATION AA-5 TRAVELER

Dimensions: Span, 31 ft 6 in (9,60 m); length, 21 ft 6 in (6,55 m); height, 6 ft 10¾ in (2,10 m); wing area, 140 sq ft (13,01 m²).

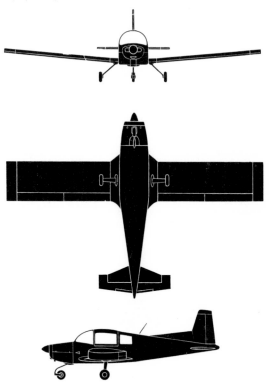

ANTONOV AN-22 ANTEI (COCK)

Country of Origin: USSR.

Type: Heavy military and commercial freighter.

Power Plant: Four 15,000 shp Kuznetsov NK-12MA turbo-props.

Performance: Max. speed, 460 mph (740 km/h); max. cruise, 422 mph (679 km/h); range with 99,208 lb (45 000 kg) payload, 6,835 mls (11 000 km) at 373 mph (600 km/h), with 176,370 lb (80 000 kg) payload, 3,107 mls (5 000 km) at 404 mph (650 km/h); cruise altitude, 26,250–32,800 ft (8 000–10 000 m).

Weights: Empty equipped, 251,327 lb (114 000 kg); max. take-off, 551,156 lb (250 000 kg).

Accommodation: Crew of five–six and cabin for 28–29 passengers between freight hold and flight deck. Freight hold can accommodate three tracked carriers for single Frog or twin Ganef surface-to-air missiles, self-propelled guns, etc.

Status: In production for both military and commercial use. First of five prototypes flown February 27, 1965, with first production deliveries following in the spring of 1967.

Notes: Capable of taking-off in fully loaded condition within 1,420 yards (1 300 m) and landing within 875 yards (800 m), the An-22 Antei (Antheus) is used extensively by the Soviet Air Forces and *Aeroflot*. The majority of An-22s now feature a reconfigured nose section (as illustrated above and on the opposite page) embodying two radars.

32

ANTONOV AN-22 ANTEI (COCK)

Dimensions: Span, 211 ft $3\frac{1}{2}$ in (64,40 m); length, 189 ft 8 in (57,80 m); height, 41 ft 1 in (12,53 m); wing area, 3,713·55 sq ft (345 m²).

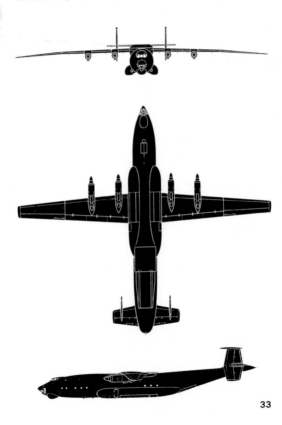

ANTONOV AN-26 (COKE)

Country of Origin: USSR.

Type: Short- to medium-range military and commercial freighter.

Power Plant: Two 2,820 eshp Ivchenko AI-24T turboprops and one (starboard nacelle) 1,984 lb (900 kg) Tumansky RU-19-300 auxiliary turbojet.

Performance: Max. speed, 335 mph (540 km/h) at 19,685 ft (6 000 m); normal cruise, 280 mph (450 km/h) at 19,685 ft (6 000 m); range cruise, 273 mph (440 km/h) at 22,965 ft (7 000 m); range with 3,307 lb (1 500 kg) payload and reserves, 1,553 mls (2 500 km), with 11,023 lb (5 000 kg) payload and reserves, 808 mls (1 300 km); service ceiling, 24,935 ft (7 600 m).

Weights: Empty equipped, 37,258 lb (16 914 kg); max. take-off, 52,911 lb (24 000 kg).

Accommodation: Normal crew of five with folding seats for up to 38 passengers/troops along main cabin walls. Direct rear loading for freight or vehicles and provision for air-dropping over rear ramp.

Status: Production deliveries for both military and commercial use reportedly commenced 1969.

Notes: Derivative of the commercial An-24RT intended for both military and civil applications, the An-26 differs from An-24 variants in having a completely redesigned rear fuselage of "beavertail" type, and large paradrop observation blister to port below and aft of the flight deck. Structurally, the An-26 is essentially similar to the An-24 Series II (see 1969 edition), and has an auxiliary turbojet in the starboard nacelle as introduced by the An-24RT.

ANTONOV AN-26 (COKE)

Dimensions: Span, 95 ft 10 in (29,20 m); length, 78 ft 1 in (23,80 m); height, 28 ft 1⅔ in (8,57 m); wing area, 779·95 sq ft (72,46 m²).

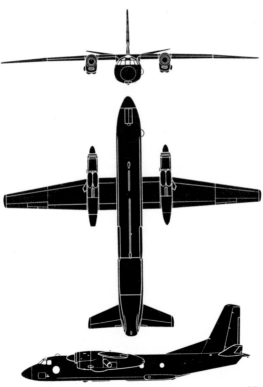

BAC LIGHTNING F. MK. 53

Country of Origin: United Kingdom.

Type: Single-seat interceptor, strike and reconnaissance fighter.

Power Plant: Two 11,100 lb (5 035 kg) dry and 16,300 lb (7 393 kg) reheat Rolls-Royce RB.146 Avon 302-C turbojets.

Performance: (Estimated in clean condition) Max. speed, 1,500 mph (2 415 km/h) or Mach 2·27 at 40,000 ft (12 190 m); long-range cruise, 595 mph (957 km/h) at 36,000–40,000 ft (10 970–12 190 m); initial climb, 50,000 ft/min (254 m/sec); time to 40,000 ft (12 190 m), 2·5 min; acceleration from Mach 1·0 to Mach 2·2, 3·5 min.

Weights: (Estimated) Max. loaded, 50,000 lb (22 680 kg).

Armament: Interchangeable packs containing equipment for two Red Top or Firestreak AAMs or 44 2-in (51-mm) rockets, plus two 30-mm Aden cannon with 120 rpg in ventral pack, plus two 1,000-lb (453,5-kg) bombs or two Matra 155 launchers for 18 68-mm SNEB rockets.

Status: First F. Mk. 53 flown November 1, 1966, and first delivery (to Saudi Arabia) December 4, 1967. Production of 34 for Saudi Arabia and 12 for Kuwait complete.

Notes: Multi-mission export version of RAF Lightning Mk. 6 interceptor, the definitive RAF single-seater. RAF received 44 Mk. 2, 58 Mk. 3 and 67 Mk. 6 single-seat Lightnings, 30 Mk. 2s having been modified as Mk. 2a version with Mk. 6 ventral pack. Two 260 Imp gal (1182 l) long-range ferry tanks may be carried on overwing pylons.

BAC LIGHTNING F. MK. 53

Dimensions: Span, 34 ft 10 in (10,61 m); length (including probe), 55 ft 3 in (16,84 m); height, 19 ft 7 in (5,97 m); approx. wing area, 460 sq ft (42,73 m²).

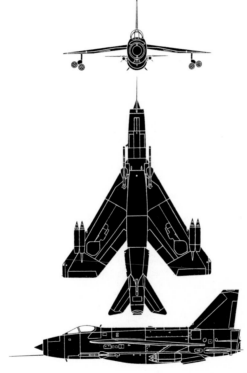

BAC ONE-ELEVEN 475

Country of Origin: United Kingdom.

Type: Short- to medium-range commercial transport.

Power Plant: Two 12,550 lb (5 692 kg) Rolls-Royce Spey 512-14-DW turbofans.

Performance: Max. cruise, 548 mph (882 km/h) at 21,000 ft (6 400 m); econ. cruise, 507 mph (815 km/h) at 25,000 ft (7 620 m); range with reserves for 230 mls (370 km) diversion and 45 min, 2,095 mls (3 370 km), with capacity payload, 1,590 mls (2 560 km); initial climb rate at 345 mph (555 km/h), 2,350 ft/min (11,93 m/sec).

Weights: Basic operational, 51,814 lb (23 502 kg); max. take-off, 92,000 lb (41 730 kg).

Accommodation: Basic flight crew of two and up to 89 passengers. Typical mixed-class arrangement provides for 16 first-class (four-abreast) and 49 tourist-class (five-abreast) passengers.

Status: Aerodynamic prototype of One-Eleven 475 flown August 27, 1970 followed by first production model on April 5, 1971, with certification and first production deliveries following in June.

Notes: The One-Eleven 475 combines the standard fuselage of the Series 400 with the redesigned wing and uprated engines of the Series 500 (see 1970 edition), coupling these with a low-pressure undercarriage to permit operation from gravel or low-strength sealed runways. The One-Eleven prototype flew on August 20, 1963, production models including the physically similar Series 200 and 300 with 10,330 lb (4 686 kg) Spey 506s and 11,400 lb (5 170 kg) Spey 511s, the Series 400 modified for US operation, and the Series 500 which is similar to the 475 apart from the fuselage.

38

BAC ONE-ELEVEN 475

Dimensions: Span, 93 ft 6 in (28,50 m); length, 93 ft 6 in (28,50 m); height, 24 ft 6 in (7,47 m); wing area, 1,031 sq ft (95,78 m²).

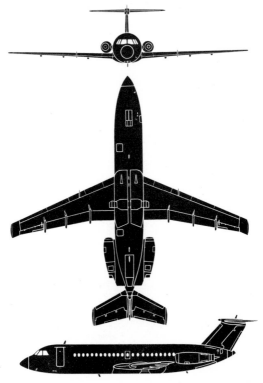

BAC 167 STRIKEMASTER

Country of Origin: United Kingdom.
Type: Side-by-side two-seat basic trainer and light attack and counter-insurgency aircraft.
Power Plant: One 3,410 lb (1 547 kg) Rolls-Royce Viper 535 turbojet.
Performance: Max. speed, 450 mph (724 km/h) at sea level, 472 mph (760 km/h) at 20,000 ft (6 096 m); range at 8,355 lb (3 789 kg), 725 mls (1 166 km), at 10,500 lb (4 762 kg), 1,238 mls (1 992 km), at 11,500 lb (5 216 kg), 1,382 mls (2 224 km); initial climb at 8,355 lb (3 789 kg), 5,250 ft/min (26,67 m/sec); time to 30,000 ft (9 150 m), 8 min 45 sec, to 40,000 ft (12 200 m), 15 min 30 sec.
Weights: Empty equipped, 5,850 lb (2 653 kg); normal take-off (pilot training), 8,355 lb (3 789 kg), (navigational training), 9,143 lb (4 147 kg); max., 11,500 lb (5 216 kg).
Armament: Provision for two 7,62-mm FN machine guns with 550 rpg and eight underwing stores stations for up to 3,000 lb (1 360 kg) of stores.
Status: Prototype Strikemaster flown October 26, 1967, with production deliveries following late 1968. Versions ordered and which differ only in equipment specified include Mk. 80 (Saudi Arabia), Mk. 81 (South Yemen), Mk. 82 (Muscat and Oman), Mk. 83 (Kuwait), Mk. 84 (Singapore), Mk. 87 (Kenya) and Mk. 88 (New Zealand). Total of 101 Strikemasters contracted for by beginning of 1972, including a batch for Ecuador.
Notes: Derivative of BAC 145 (see 1971 edition) from which it differs primarily in having a more powerful engine, some local structural strengthening, and additional stores stations.

40

BAC 167 STRIKEMASTER

Dimensions: Span, 35 ft 4 in (10,77 m); length, 34 ft 0 in (10,36 m); height, 10 ft 2 in (3,10 m); wing area, 213·7 sq ft (19,80 m²).

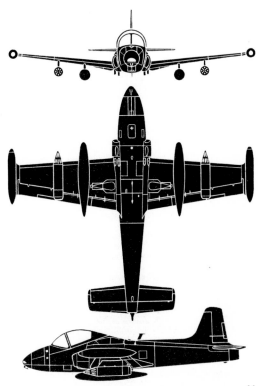

BAC-AÉROSPATIALE CONCORDE

Countries of Origin: United Kingdom and France.
Type: Long-range supersonic commercial transport.
Power Plant: Four 38,050 lb (17 259 kg) reheat Rolls-Royce/SNECMA Olympus 602 turbojets.
Performance: Max. cruise, 1,450 mph (2 330 km/h) or Mach 2·2 at 54,500 ft (16 000 m); max. range cruise, 1,350 mph (2 170 km/h) or Mach 2·05; max. fuel range with FAR reserves and 17,000-lb (7 710-kg) payload, 4,400 mls (7 080 km); max. payload range, 3,600 mls (5 790 km) at 616 mph (990 km/h) or Mach 0·93 at 30,000 ft (9 100 m), 4,020 mls (6 470 km) at 1,350 mph (2 170 km/h) or Mach 2·05 at 54,500 ft (16 000 m); initial climb, 5,000 ft/min (25,4 m/sec).
Weights: Operational empty, 169,000 lb (76 650 kg); max. take-off, 385,000 lb (90 720 kg).
Accommodation: Normal flight crew of three and economy-class seating for 128 passengers. Alternative high-density arrangement for 144 passengers.
Status: First and second prototypes flown March 2 and April 9, 1969 respectively. First of two pre-production aircraft flew December 17, 1971, the second being scheduled for September 1972, and first production aircraft following in December 1972.
Notes: Both specification and general-arrangement silhouette apply to production Concorde, the prototypes featuring a shorter fuselage and differences in cockpit visor and wing profile. The Concorde reached Mach 2·0 on November 4, 1970, the prototypes having 34,700 lb (15 740 kg) Olympus 593-3Bs, and the definitive engine for the production model will be the Olympus 612 of 38,400 lb (17 418 kg). Ten production Concordes were under construction by beginning of 1972.

42

BAC-AÉROSPATIALE CONCORDE

Dimensions: Span, 84 ft 0 in (25,60 m); length, 203 ft $8\frac{3}{4}$ in (62,10 m); height, 39 ft $10\frac{1}{4}$ in (12,15 m); wing area, 3,856 sq ft (358,25 m^2).

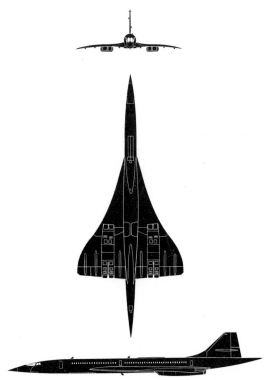

BEECHCRAFT 99A

Country of Origin: USA.

Type: Light commercial feederliner.

Power Plant: Two 680 shp Pratt & Whitney PT6A-27 turboprops.

Performance: Max. cruise, 284 mph (457 km/h) at 12,000 ft (3 650 m); econ. cruise, 279 mph (449 km/h) at 8,000 ft (2 440 m); range cruise, 216 mph (348 km/h) at 8,000 ft (2 440 m); max. fuel range, 887 mls (1 427 km) at 8,000 ft (2 440 m) with 45 min reserves at 279 mph (449 km/h), 1,048 mls (1 686 km) at 216 mph (348 km/h); initial climb, 1,700 ft/min (8,6 m/sec); service ceiling, 26,200 ft (7 985 m).

Weights: Empty equipped (standard 15-seater), 5,780 lb (2 621 kg); max. take-off, 10,400 lb (4 717 kg).

Accommodation: Normal flight crew of two and 15 passengers in individual seats on each side of central aisle. Optional 8-seat business executive transport arrangement. An 800-lb (363-kg) capacity ventral cargo pod (shown fitted above and on opposite page) may be carried.

Status: The prototype Model 99 was flown in July 1966 and the first production delivery followed on May 2, 1968, the 100th being delivered on April 28, 1969. The 36th production Model 99 served as a prototype for the Model 99A, deliveries of which began in 1969, and both versions remained in production at the beginning of 1972.

Notes: Standard Model 99 has 550 shp PT6A-20 turboprops. Installation of a forward-hinged cargo door forward of the standard air-stair door to permit all-cargo or mixed passenger-cargo operation is optional.

BEECHCRAFT 99A

Dimensions: Span, 45 ft 10½ in (14,00 m); length, 44 ft 6¾ in (13,58 m); height, 14 ft 4⅓ in (4,40 m); wing area, 279·7 sq ft (25,985 m²).

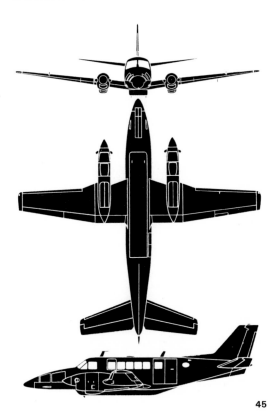

BEECHCRAFT KING AIR A100

Country of Origin: USA.

Type: Light commercial feederliner and business executive transport.

Power Plant: Two 680 shp Pratt & Whitney PT6A-28 turboprops.

Performance: Max. cruise, 285 mph (459 km/h) at 10,000 ft (3 048 m), 280 mph (451 km/h) at 16,000 ft (4 877 m), 270 mph (434 km/h) at 21,000 ft (6 400 m); range, 1,326 mls (2 138 km) at 10,000 ft (3 048 m), 1,464 mls (2 356 km) at 16,000 ft (4 877 m), 1,542 mls (2 482 km); service ceiling at 11,500 lb/5 217 kg, 24,850 ft (7 575 m).

Weights: Empty equipped, 6,728 lb (3 052 kg); max. take-off, 11,500 lb (5 217 kg).

Accommodation: Normal flight crew of two and seating for six passengers in standard business executive configuration. Variety of alternative cabin configurations including 15-seat feederliner version.

Status: King Air A100 introduced August 1971 as production successor to King Air 100 (see 1970 edition).

Notes: The King Air A100 differs from the predecessing production model in having increased fuel capacity and increased take-off and payload weights. The King Air 100 was the third generation development of the King Air series, with lengthened fuselage, enlarged vertical tail, dual wheel main undercarriage members and more powerful PT6A-28 turboprops.

46

BEECHCRAFT KING AIR A100

Dimensions: Span, 45 ft 10½ in (13,98 m); length, 39 ft 8½ in (12,10 m); height, 15 ft 4¼ in (4,68 m); wing area, 277·06 sq ft (25,74 m²).

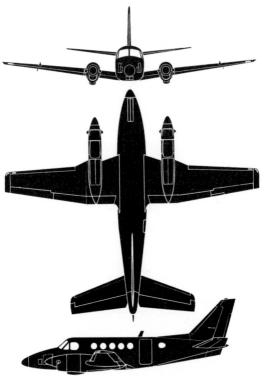

BERIEV BE-12 TCHAIKA (MAIL)

Country of Origin: USSR.

Type: Maritime patrol and reconnaissance amphibian.

Power Plant: Two 4,190 eshp Ivchenko AI-20D turboprops.

Performance: (Estimated) Max. speed, 380 mph (610 km/h) at 10,000 ft (3 050 m); max. cruise, 340 mph (547 km/h) at 15,000 ft (4 570 m); normal patrol speed, 200–250 mph (320–400 km/h) at 5,000 ft (1 525 m); initial climb at normal loaded weight, 3,000 ft/min (15,2 m/sec); service ceiling, 37,000 ft (11 280 m); max. range, 2,500 mls (4 025 km).

Weights: (Estimated) Max. take-off, 60,000–65,000 lb (27 220–29 485 kg).

Armament: Underwing stores stations for homing torpedoes, depth bombs, mines or rockets. Internal stowage for sonobuoys.

Status: Reportedly flown in prototype form in 1960, the Be-12 is believed to have entered service with the Soviet Navy during 1965–66.

Notes: The largest amphibian flying boat currently in service, the Be-12 Tchaika (Gull) is standard equipment with the Soviet Navy maritime patrol units and established a number of FAI-recognised records for aircraft in its class during 1964–70. The Be-12 serves in substantial numbers from Northern and Black Sea Fleet air bases, and is also operating over the Mediterranean from Egyptian bases.

BERIEV BE-12 TCHAIKA (MAIL)

Dimensions: (Estimated) Span, 108 ft 0 in (32,9 m); length, 96 ft 0 in (29,26 m); height, 23 ft 0 in (7,01 m); wing area, 1,030 sq ft (95,69 m²).

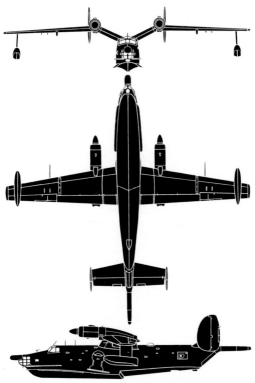

49

BERIEV BE-30 (CUFF)

Country of Origin: USSR.

Type: Light short-range commercial feederliner.

Power Plant: Two 970 eshp Glushenkov TVD-10 turbo-props.

Performance: Max. speed, 304 mph (490 km/h); max. cruise, 286 mph (460 km/h) at 6,500 ft (1 980 m); range with 1,984-lb (900-kg) payload and 30 min reserves, 620 mls (1 000 km) at 236 mph (380 km/h), with 2,755-lb (1 250-kg) payload, 373 mls (600 km).

Weights: Empty equipped, 7,937 lb (3 600 kg); max. take-off, 12,919 lb (5 860 kg).

Accommodation: Normal flight crew of two and standard arrangement for 14 passengers in pairs in individual seats on each side of central aisle. Proposed high-density arrangements for 21–23 passengers.

Status: First prototype Be-30 flown (with ASh-21 piston engines) on March 3, 1967, followed by definitive series prototype on July 18, 1968. The Be-30 entered service with *Aeroflot* during the course of 1970.

Notes: Designed specifically for use by *Aeroflot* over local service routes not justifying use of the larger An-24, and capable of operating from short grass strips or gravel runways, the Be-30 is also being developed for geological survey and other tasks. It is also convertible for use as a freighter or air ambulance, accommodating nine stretcher cases and six seated casualties in the latter role.

BERIEV BE-30 (CUFF)

Dimensions: Span, 55 ft 9¼ in (17,00 m); length, 51 ft 6 in (15,70 m); height, 17 ft 0¾ in (5,20 m); wing area, 344·445 sq ft (32,0 m²).

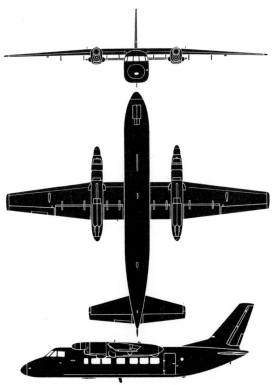

BOEING MODEL 727-100C

Country of Origin: USA.

Type: Medium-range commercial convertible cargo-passenger transport.

Power Plant: Three 14,000 lb (6 350 kg) Pratt & Whitney JT8D-7 turbofans.

Performance: Max. speed, 630 mph (1 014 km/h) at 21,600 ft (6 585 m); max. cruise, 605 mph (974 km/h) at 19,000 ft (5 800 m); econ. cruise, 570 mph (917 km/h) at 30,000 ft (9 150 m); range with max. fuel, 2,650 mls (4 265 km), with max. payload, 1,900 mls (3 058 km); initial climb, 3,150 ft/min (16 m/sec); service ceiling, 37,400 ft (11 400 m).

Weights: Operational empty, 89,537 lb (40 613 kg); standard max. take-off, 160,000 lb (72 570 kg); optional max. take-off, 169,000 lb (76 655 kg).

Accommodation: Normal flight crew of three. Typical payloads comprise 94 mixed-class passengers, 52 passengers plus 22,700 lb (10 295 kg) of cargo, or 38,000 lb (17 236 kg) of cargo. Conversion from mixed passenger/cargo to all-cargo configuration is possible in less than two hours.

Status: First Model 727-100 flown February 9, 1963, first delivery (to United) following on October 29, 1963. Model 727-200 (see 1970 edition) flown July 27, 1967, with first delivery following (to Northeast) on December 11, 1967. Approximately 865 of all versions delivered by beginning of 1972 against total orders for 893.

Notes: Model 727-100C is identical to -100 apart from strengthened freight floor and cargo door. The -100QC uses palletised passenger seats and galleys.

BOEING MODEL 727-100C

Dimensions: Span, 108 ft 0 in (32,92 m); length, 133 ft 2 in (40,59 m); height, 34 ft 0 in (10,36 m); wing area, 1,700 sq ft (157,9 m²).

BOEING MODEL 737-200C

Country of Origin: USA.

Type: Short-range commercial convertible cargo–passenger transport.

Power Plant: Two 14,500 lb (6 575 kg) Pratt & Whitney JT8D-9 turbofans.

Performance: Max. speed, 586 mph (943 km/h) at 23,500 ft (7 165 m); max. cruise, 568 mph (915 km/h) at 21,900 ft (6 675 m); econ. cruise, 525 mph (845 km/h) at 30,000 ft (9 145 m); range with max. fuel and reserves for 200-mile diversion and 45 min, 2,210 mls (3 555 km), max. payload and similar reserves, 2,135 mls (3 435 km).

Weights: Operational empty (all cargo), 59,109 lb (26 805 kg), (all passenger), 62,436 lb (28 315 kg); max. take-off, 114,500 lb (51 925 kg).

Accommodation: Normal flight crew of two and up to 119 passengers in six-abreast seating in all-passenger configuration, or up to 34,270 lb (15 544 kg) in cargo configuration.

Status: First Model 737-100 flown on April 9, 1967 (see 1967 edition), followed by first -200 on August 8, 1967. Approximately 288 Model 737s of all versions delivered by beginning of 1972 against total orders for 325.

Notes: All aircraft delivered since May 1971 have been completed to the so-called "Advanced 737-200/C/QC" standard (to which specification refers), embodying improvements in range and short-field performance, and the first example with 15,500 lb (7 030 kg) JT8D-15 engines was scheduled for March 1972 delivery (to Saudi Arabian Airlines).

BOEING MODEL 737-200C

Dimensions: Span, 93 ft 0 in (28,35 m); length, 100 ft 0 in (30,48 m); height, 37 ft 0 in (11,28 m); wing area, 980 sq ft (91,05 m²).

BOEING MODEL 747B

Country of Origin: USA.

Type: Long-range large-capacity commercial transport.

Power Plant: Four 45,000 lb (20 410 kg) Pratt & Whitney JT9D-3W turbofans.

Performance: Max. speed at 600,000 lb (272 155 kg), 608 mph (978 km/h) at 30,000 ft (9 150 m); long-range cruise, 589 mph (948 km/h) at 35,000 ft (10 670 m); range with max. fuel and FAR reserves, 7,080 mls (11 395 km), with 79,618-lb (36 114-kg) payload, 6,620 mls (10 650 km); cruise ceiling, 45,000 ft (13 715 m).

Weights: Operational empty, 361,216 lb (163 844 kg); max. take-off, 775,000 lb (351 540 kg).

Accommodation: Normal flight crew of three and basic accommodation for 66 first-class and 308 economy-class passengers. Alternative layouts for 447 or 490 economy-class passengers in nine-abreast and 10-abreast seating respectively.

Status: First Model 747-100 flown on February 9, 1969, and first commercial services (by Pan American) inaugurated January 22, 1970. The first Model 747-200 (747B), the 88th aircraft off the assembly line, flown October 11, 1970.

Notes: Principal production versions of the Model 747 are currently the -100 and -200 series, the latter having greater fuel capacity and increased maximum take-off weight, convertible passenger/cargo and all-cargo versions of the -200 series (alias Model 747B) being designated 747C and 747F respectively. The first production example of the latter flew on November 30, 1971, and was scheduled for delivery (to Lufthansa) during March 1972.

BOEING MODEL 747B

Dimensions: Span, 195 ft 8 in (59,64 m); length, 231 ft 4 in (70,51 m); height, 63 ft 5 in (19,33 m); wing area, 5,685 sq ft (528,15 m²).

BREGUET 1150 ATLANTIC

Country of Origin: France.

Type: Long-range maritime patrol aircraft.

Power Plant: Two 6,105 ehp Hispano-built Rolls-Royce Tyne R.Ty.20 Mk. 21 turboprops.

Performance: Max. speed, 409 mph (658 km/h); max. cruise, 363 mph (584 km/h) at 19,685 ft (6 000 m), 342 mph (550 km/h) at 26,250 ft (8 000 m); range cruise, 311 mph (500 km/h) at 26,250 ft (8 000 m); max. endurance cruise, 195 mph (320 km/h); loiter endurance at range of 620 mls (1 000 km), 12 hrs; max. endurance, 18 hrs; range with 10% reserves, 4,950 mls (7 970 km); max. range, 5,590 mls (9 000 km); initial climb, 2,450 ft/min (12,44 m/sec); service ceiling, 32,800 ft (10 000 m).

Weights: Empty, 52,900 lb (24 000 kg); max. take-off, 95,900 lb (43 500 kg).

Armament: Nine 400-lb (181,4-kg) Mk. 44 acoustic torpedoes or four 1,124-lb (510-kg) L4 torpedoes plus single nuclear depth charge internally, and four AS.12 missiles beneath wings.

Accommodation: Crew of 12 of which seven accommodated in central operations compartment.

Status: First of three prototypes flown October 21, 1961, and production against total orders for 87 (40 for France, 20 for Germany, 18 for Italy and nine for the Netherlands) scheduled to continue until early 1973.

Notes: Built by French-German-Belgian-Italian-Dutch consortium with final assembly in France.

58

BREGUET 1150 ATLANTIC

Dimensions: Span, 119 ft $1\frac{1}{4}$ in (36,30 m); length, 104 ft $1\frac{1}{2}$ in (31,75 m); height, 37 ft $1\frac{3}{4}$ in (11,33 m); wing area, 1,295·33 sq ft (120,34 m²).

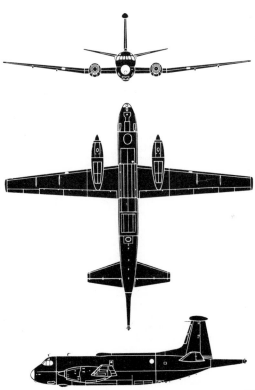

BRITTEN-NORMAN BN-2A ISLANDER

Country of Origin: United Kingdom.
Type: Light utility transport.
Power Plant: Two 260 hp Lycoming O-540-E4C5 six-cylinder horizontally-opposed engines.
Performance: Max. speed, 170 mph (273 km/h) at sea level; cruise at 75% power, 160 mph (257 km/h) at 7,000 ft (2 140 m), at 67% power, 158 mph (253 km/h) at 9,000 ft (2 750 m), at 59% power, 154 mph (248 km/h) at 13,000 ft (3 960 m); range with standard fuel, 717 mls (1 154 km) at 160 mph (257 km/h), 870 mls (1 400 km) at 154 mph (248 km/h), with tip tanks, 1,040 mls (1 674 km) at 160 mph (257 km/h), 1,263 mls (2 035 km) at 154 mph (248 km/h); initial climb, 1,050 ft/min (5,3 m/sec); service ceiling, 14,600 ft (4 450 m).
Weights: Empty equipped, 3,588 lb (1 627 kg) max. Take-off, 6,300 lb (2 857 kg).
Accommodation: Flight crew of one or two and 8–9 passengers on bench-type seats, or two casualty stretchers and two attendants for ambulance role.
Status: Prototype flown June 12, 1965, followed by first production aircraft on August 20, 1966 and 300th delivered in August 1971. Two hundred and fifteen airframes being manufactured under contract by IRMA in Rumania. Production rate of three per month being maintained at beginning of 1972 by Britten-Norman (Bembridge) Ltd.
Notes: Military version known as Defender with four underwing stores pylons and nose-mounted weather radar for search and rescue missions, anti-smuggling patrols, etc.

BRITTEN-NORMAN BN-2A ISLANDER

Dimensions: Span, 49 ft 0 in (14,94 m); length, 35 ft 8 in (10,87 m); height, 13 ft 8 in (4,16 m); wing area, 325 sq ft (30,2 m²).

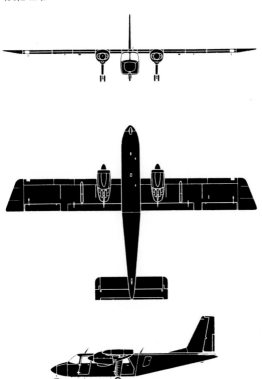

BRITTEN-NORMAN BN-2A MK III
TRISLANDER

Country of Origin: United Kingdom.
Type: Light utility transport and feederliner.
Power Plant: Three 260 hp Lycoming O-540-E4C5 six-cylinder horizontally-opposed engines.
Performance: Max. speed, 187 mph (301 km/h) at sea level; cruise at 75% power, 180 mph (290 km/h) at 6,500 ft (1 980 m), at 67% power, 175 mph (282 km/h) at 9,000 ft (2 750 m), at 59% power, 170 mph (274 km/h) at 13,000 ft (3 960 m); range with max. payload, 160 mls (257 km) at 170 mph (274 km/h), with 2,400-lb (1 089-kg) payload, 700 mls (1 127 km) at 175 mph (282 km/h); initial climb, 1,120 ft/min (5,7 m/sec); service ceiling, 14,500 ft (4 420 m).
Weights: Empty equipped, 5,638 lb (2 557 kg); max. take-off, 9,350 lb (4 240 kg).
Accommodation: Flight crew of one or two, and 16–17 passengers in pairs on bench-type seats.
Status: Prototype flown September 11, 1970, with production prototype flying on March 6, 1971. First production Trislander flown April 29, 1971, and first delivery (to Aurigny) following on June 29, 1971. One Trislander per month being produced by Britten-Norman (Bembridge) Ltd. at beginning of 1972.
Notes: The Trislander is a derivative of the Islander (see pages 60–61) with which it has 75% commonality. The wingtip auxiliary fuel tanks optional on the Islander have been standardised for the Trislander.

BRITTEN-NORMAN BN-2A MK III TRISLANDER

Dimensions: Span, 53 ft 0 in (16,15 m); length, 43 ft 9 in (13,33 m); height, 13 ft $5\frac{3}{4}$ in (4,11 m); wing area, 337 sq ft (31,25 m²).

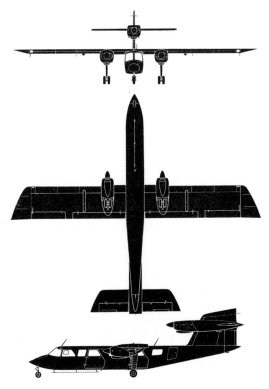

CASA C.212 AVIOCAR

Country of Origin: Spain.

Type: STOL utility transport.

Power Plant: Two 755 eshp Garrett-AiResearch TPE-331-201 turboprops.

Performance: Max. speed, 236 mph (380 km/h) at 12,000 ft (3 660 m); max. cruise, 228 mph (367 km/h) at 12,000 ft (3 660 m); econ. cruise, 177 mph (285 km/h) at 10,000 ft (3 050 m); range with max. fuel and 5% plus 30 min reserves, 1,295 mls (2 085 km) at 9,840 ft (3 000 m), with max. payload and same reserves, 445 mls (720 km); initial climb, 1,655 ft/min (8,4 m/sec); service ceiling, 23,950 ft (7 300 m).

Weights: Empty equipped, 7,160 lb (3 250 kg); max. take-off, 13,230 lb (6 000 kg).

Accommodation: Flight crew of two and (commercial version) 18 passengers with alternative high-density arrangement for 21 passengers. Ten casualty stretchers, three sitting casualties plus medical attendants may be accommodated for the ambulance role, and the military version will carry 15 paratroops and a jumpmaster.

Status: Two prototypes flown March 26 and October 23, 1971, and contract awarded in 1971 for 50 examples for the Spanish Air Force with deliveries commencing in 1973.

Notes: The Aviocar has been designed primarily for operation by the Spanish Air Force, and is expected to replace the aged Junkers Ju 52/3m from 1974. The Aviocar features a rear loading ramp which may be opened in flight for paradrops. The wing centre section, engine nacelles and flaps are to be manufactured in Germany by MBB.

CASA C.212 AVIOCAR

Dimensions: Span, 62 ft 4 in (19,00 m); length, 49 ft $8\frac{1}{2}$ in (15,15 m); height, 20 ft $8\frac{3}{4}$ in (6,32 m); wing area, 430·556 sq ft (40,0 m²).

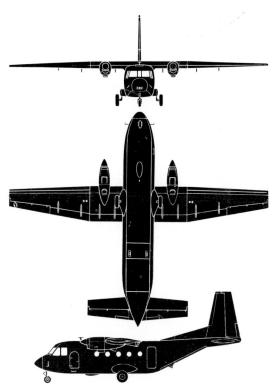

CESSNA MODEL 500 CITATION

Country of Origin: USA.

Type: Light business executive transport.

Power Plant: Two 2,200 lb (1 000 kg) Pratt & Whitney JT15D-1 turbofans.

Performance: Max. speed, 402 mph (647 km/h) at 26,400 ft (8 046 m); max. cruise, 400 mph (644 km/h) at 25,400 ft (7 740 m); range with eight persons and 45 min reserves at 90% cruise thrust, 1,397 mls (2 248 km), with two persons and same reserves at 90% cruise thrust, 1,502 mls (2 417 km); initial climb, 3,350 ft/min (17 m/sec); service ceiling, 38,400 ft (11 704 m).

Weights: Empty (excluding avionics), 5,408 lb (2 453 kg); max. take-off, 10,850 lb (4 921 kg).

Accommodation: Crew of two on separate flight deck and alternative arrangements for five or six passengers in main cabin.

Status: First of two prototypes flown on September 15, 1969, and first production Citation flown in May 1971. Customer deliveries began in October 1971 with 60–80 to be completed during first year of production.

Notes: The Citation places emphasis on short-field performance, balanced field length being 2,950 ft (899 m) and take-off distance to clear a 35-ft (10,7-m) obstacle being 2,300 ft (701 m), enabling the aircraft to use some 2,300 US airfields. The Citation is being offered in basic standard configuration or as a complete business aircraft package with factory-installed interior and avionics, ground and flight training and one year of maintenance service.

CESSNA MODEL 500 CITATION

Dimensions: Span, 43 ft 8½ in (13,32 m); length, 43 ft 6 in (13,26 m); height, 14 ft 3¾ in (4,36 m); wing area, 260 sq ft (24,15 m²).

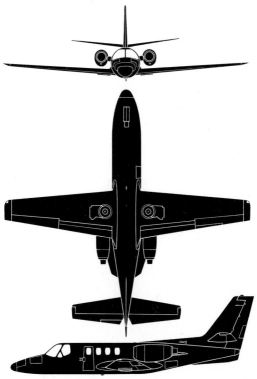

CONVAIR (GENERAL DYNAMICS) F-111E

Country of Origin: USA.
Type: Two-seat tactical strike fighter.
Power Plant: Two 19,600 lb (8 890 kg) reheat Pratt & Whitney TF30-P-9 turbofans.
Performance: Max. speed, 865 mph (1 390 km/h) or Mach 1·2 at sea level, 1,650 mph (2 655 km/h) or Mach 2·5 at 40,000 ft (12 190 m); ferry range with max. internal fuel, 3,800 mls (6 115 km); tactical radius with 16,000-lb (7 257-kg) combat load for hi-lo-hi mission profile, 1,500 mls (2 415 km); approx. max. climb at 74,000 lb (33 566 kg), 40,000 ft/min (203,2 m/sec).
Weights: Empty operational, 47,500 lb (23 525 kg); normal take-off, 74,000 lb (33 566 kg); max. overload take-off, 91,500 lb (41 504 kg).
Armament: One 20-mm M-61A1 rotary cannon with 2,000 rounds or two 750-lb M117 bombs internally. Approx. max. ordnance load of 30,000 lb (13 608 kg) for short-range interdiction. External ordnance carried by four 4,000-lb (1 814-kg) swivelling wing stations and four fixed stations.
Status: First of 28 test and development F-111s flown December 21, 1964. Initial production model, the F-111A (see 1969 edition), of which 141 built. Superseded by F-111E (94 aircraft) from late 1969, these being followed by F-111D (96 aircraft) and F-111F (70 aircraft), with production phase-out late 1972.
Notes: F-111E differs from F-111A in having revised air intake geometry and TF30-P-9 turbofans, and the similarly-powered F-111D features more advanced avionics. The F-111F has TF30-P-100 engines and simplified avionics.

68

CONVAIR (GENERAL DYNAMICS) F-111E

Dimensions: Span (max.), 63 ft 0 in (19,20 m), (min.),
31 ft 11⅓ in (9,74); length, 73 ft 6 in (22,40 m); height,
17 ft 1⅓ in (5,22 m).

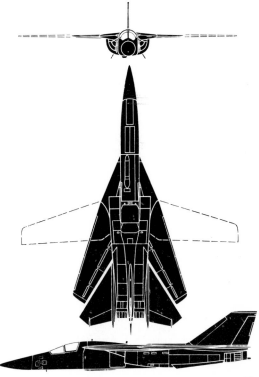

CONVAIR (GENERAL DYNAMICS) FB-111A

Country of Origin: USA.

Type: Two-seat strategic bomber.

Power Plant: Two 20,500 lb (9 295 kg) reheat Pratt & Whitney TF30-P-7 turbofans.

Performance: Max. speed in clean configuration, 838 mph (1 350 km/h) or Mach 1·1 at sea level, 1,450 mph (2 334 km/h) or Mach 2·2 at 40,000 ft (12 190 m); tactical radius with subsonic cruise to target, supersonic approach and escape, and return at subsonic cruise, carrying four SRAM to target, 1,200 mls (1 930 km); ferry range with four 500 Imp gal (2 273 l) external tanks, 4,100 mls (6 600 km); service ceiling, 65,000 ft (19 810 m).

Weights: (Estimated) Max. take-off, 100,000 lb (45 360 kg).

Armament: Up to six 2,200-lb (998-kg) Boeing AGM-69A short-range attack missiles (SRAM) on external pylons, or conventional ordnance loads up to 37,500 lb (16 010 kg). Typical short-range interdiction load comprises 50 750-lb (340-kg) bombs on multiple ejection racks.

Status: First FB-111A flown July 13, 1968, first delivery to USAF following October 8, 1969. Production against orders for 76 aircraft was completed during the course of 1971.

Notes: The FB-111A airframe is essentially similar to that of the F-111E (see pages 68–69), but employs the long-span wings originally developed for the F-111B (see 1966 edition) and a new undercarriage. Full load of 750-lb (340-kg) bombs is carried with wings swept at 26 degrees, reducing to 38 bombs at 54 degrees of sweep or 20 bombs at maximum sweep.

CONVAIR (GENERAL DYNAMICS) FB-111A

Dimensions: Span (max.), 70 ft 0 in (21,34 m), (min.), 33 ft 11 in (10,34 m); length, 73 ft 6 in (22,40 m); height, 17 ft 1½ in (5,22 m).

F-WTAL

DASSAULT/BREGUET FALCON 10

Country of Origin: France.

Type: Light business executive transport.

Power Plant: Two 3,230 lb (1 465 kg) Garrett-AiResearch TFE-731-2 turbofans.

Performance: Max. cruise, 572 mph (920 km/h) at 30,000 ft (9 145 m); range with four passengers and 45 min reserves, 2,475 mls (3 980 km), with seven passengers, 1,993 mls (3 208 km).

Weights: Empty equipped, 9,863 lb (4 474 kg); max. takeoff, 18,298 lb (8 300 kg).

Accommodation: Flight crew of two and normal seating for seven or nine passengers.

Status: First prototype flown December 1, 1970, followed by second prototype on October 15, 1971. Deliveries of production aircraft scheduled to commence mid-1972.

Notes: The Falcon 10 is basically a scaled-down version of the Falcon 20 (see pages 74–75), and is currently being offered in two versions, the Falcon 10A with accommodation for seven passengers and the Falcon 10B with accommodation for nine passengers and with an additional window in each side of the cabin. An alternative executive layout for four passengers is available, and a military crew training and liaison model is competing with the Aérospatiale SN 600 Corvette (see pages 18–19) to fulfil an *Armée de l'Air* requirement, an order for some 45 examples of the selected aircraft being anticipated.

DASSAULT/BREGUET FALCON 10

Dimensions: Span, 43 ft 0 in (13,10 m); length, 44 ft 11 in (13,69 m); height, 14 ft 3 in (4,37 m); wing area, 242·19 sq ft (22,5 m²).

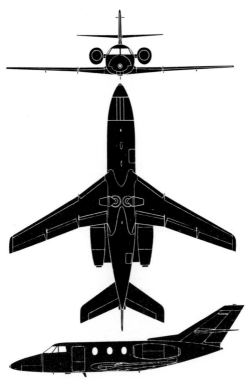

DASSAULT/BREGUET FALCON 20 SERIES F

Country of Origin: France.
Type: Light business executive transport.
Power Plant: Two 4,315 lb (1 983 kg) General Electric CF700-2D-2 turbofans.
Performance: Max. speed, 404 mph (650 km/h) at sea level, 449 mph (722 km/h) at 22,965 ft (7 000 m); max. cruise, 535 mph (860 km/h); range with eight passengers and 45 min reserves, 2,300 mls (3 580 km) at 39,370 ft (12 000 m); max. operating altitude, 42,650 ft (13 000 m).
Weights: Empty, 15,972 lb (7 245 kg); max. take-off, 28,660 lb (13 000 kg).
Accommodation: Normal flight crew of two and standard arrangement for eight passengers in individual seats. Alternative arrangements available for 10–14 passengers.
Status: First Falcon 20 (alias Mystère 20) flown May 4, 1963, followed by first production aircraft on January 1, 1965. The prototype Series F (172nd airframe) flown May 1969 and first production example of this series delivered June 1970.
Notes: Current production version of the Falcon 20, the Series F, differs from the Series E that it supplants in having wing high-lift devices to reduce field length and increased fuel tankage. A development of the Series F using the same wing and power plants, the Falcon 20T, is scheduled to commence its flight test programme in July 1972. This features a lengthened fuselage of increased cross section, and will have three-abreast seating for 26 passengers. Production deliveries of the Falcon 20T are expected to commence in 1973.

DASSAULT/BREGUET FALCON 20 SERIES F

Dimensions: Span, 53 ft 6 in (16,30 m); length, 56 ft 3 in (17,15 m); height, 17 ft 5 in (5,32 m); wing area, 440 sq ft (41 m²).

DASSAULT/BREGUET MERCURE

Country of Origin: France.
Type: Short-range commercial transport.
Power Plant: Two 15,500 lb (7 030 kg) Pratt & Whitney JT8D-15 turbofans.
Performance: Max. cruise, 581 mph (935 km/h) at 20,000 ft (6 100 m); econ. cruise, 575 mph (925 km/h) at 25,000 ft (7 620 m); range cruise, 512 mph (825 km/h) at 35,100 ft (10 700 m); range with max. payload, 466 mls (750 km), with max. fuel, 1,025 mls (1 650 km); initial climb, 2,940 ft/min (14,9 m/sec).
Weights: Operational empty, 63,713 lb (28 900 kg); max. take-off, 114,640 lb (52 000 kg).
Accommodation: Normal flight crew of two and typical mixed-class accommodation for 124 passengers (12 in four-abreast and 112 in five- and six-abreast seating) or 134 passengers in all-tourist class configuration. High-density arrangement for up to 155 passengers.
Status: First of two prototypes flown on May 28, 1971, with second prototype scheduled to fly in July 1972. First production deliveries (to Air Inter) planned for April 1974.
Notes: The Mercure is optimised for very short ranges, and some 30 per cent of the launching cost is being shared by Aeritalia in Italy (which will manufacture the tail unit and tail cone), CASA in Spain (which will manufacture the first and second fuselage sections), SABCA in Belgium (which will build the flaps, ailerons, spoilers and air brakes), and FW in Switzerland (which will produce the engine air intakes and cowling panels). The first prototype is powered by 15,000 lb (6 805 kg) JT8D-11 turbofans.

DASSAULT/BREGUET MERCURE

Dimensions: Span, 100 ft 3 in (30,55 m); length, 111 ft 6 in (34,00 m); height, 37 3$\frac{1}{4}$ in (11,36 m); wing area, 1,250 sq ft (116 m²).

DASSAULT/BREGUET MILAN S

Country of Origin: France.

Type: Single-seat multi-purpose fighter.

Power Plant: One 11,023 lb (5 000 kg) dry and 15,873 lb (7 200 kg) reheat SNECMA Atar 9K-50 turbojet.

Performance: Max. speed (clean), 865 mph (1 390 km/h) or Mach 1·14 at sea level, 1,450 mph (2 335 km/h) or Mach 2·2 at 39,370 ft (12 000 m); max. low-altitude penetration speed with typical external ordnance load, 690 mph (1 110 km/h) or Mach 0·9; time to 50,000 ft (15 250 m) at Mach 1·8, 4 min; max. initial climb, 40,160 ft/min (204 m/sec).

Weights: Loaded (clean), 21,384 lb (9 700 kg); max. take-off, 30,864 lb (14 000 kg).

Armament: Two 30-mm DEFA cannon with 125 rpg and seven external ordnance stations. Maximum external load (ordnance and fuel), 9,260 lb (4 200 kg).

Status: Prototype flown May 29, 1970. Series production aircraft available from 1972.

Notes: The Milan (Kite) is a derivative of the Mirage 5 (see pages 80–81) from which it differs primarily in having a more powerful turbojet, a controllable canard, or foreplane, which improves take-off and landing performance, and subsonic manoeuvrability, and a navigational-attack system similar to that of the Jaguar. The Milan S was competing with the Vought A-7G for Swiss orders in April–May 1972.

DASSAULT/BREGUET MILAN S

Dimensions: Span, 26 ft 11½ in (8,22 m); length, 49 ft 3½ in (15,03 m); height, 13 ft 11½ in (4,25 m); wing area, 375·12 sq ft (34,85 m²).

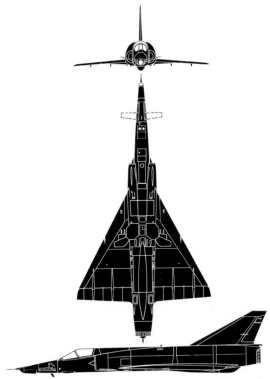

DASSAULT/BREGUET MIRAGE 5

Country of Origin: France.

Type: Single-seat ground attack fighter.

Power Plant: One 9,436 lb (4 280 kg) dry and 13,670 lb (6 200 kg) reheat SNECMA Atar 9C turbojet.

Performance: Max. speed (clean), 835 mph (1 335 km/h) or Mach 1·1 at sea level, 1,386 mph (2 230 km/h) or Mach 2·1 at 39,370 ft (12 000 m); cruise, 594 mph (956 km/h) at 36,090 ft (11 000 m); combat radius with 2,000-lb (907-kg) bomb load (hi-lo-hi profile), 805 mls (1 300 km), (lo-lo-lo profile), 400 mls (650 km); ferry range with max. external fuel, 2,485 mls (4 000 km); time to 36,090 ft (11 000 m) at Mach 0·9, 3 min, to 49,210 ft (15 000 m) at Mach 1·8, 6 min 50 sec.

Weights: Empty equipped, 14,550 lb (6 600 kg); max. loaded, 29,760 lb (13 500 kg).

Armament: Two 30-mm DEFA 5-52 cannon with 125 rpg and seven external ordnance stations. Maximum external load (ordnance and fuel), 9,260 lb (4 200 kg).

Status: Prototype flown May 19, 1967, and first deliveries (to Peru) following May 1968. Assembly (for Belgian Air Force) being undertaken in Belgium by SABCA.

Notes: The Mirage 5 is an export version of the Mirage IIIE (see 1967 edition) optimised for the ground attack role and featuring simplified avionics. Orders at beginning of 1972 included 30 for Pakistan, 16 for Peru (including two two-seaters, one of which is illustrated above), 14 for Colombia (plus four two-seat Mirage IIIs), 106 for Belgium (including 16 two-seaters and 63 for tac-recce role), and 110 for Libya (including 10 two-seaters).

DASSAULT/BREGUET MIRAGE 5

Dimensions: Span, 26 ft 11½ in (8,22 m); length, 51 ft 0¼ in (15,55 m); height, 13 ft 11½ in (4,25 m); wing area, 375·12 sq ft (34,85 m²).

DASSAULT/BREGUET MIRAGE F1

Country of Origin: France.

Type: Single-seat multi-purpose fighter.

Power Plant: One 11,023 lb (5 000 kg) dry and 15,873 lb (7 200 kg) reheat SNECMA Atar 9K-50 turbojet.

Performance: Max. speed (clean), 915 mph (1 472 km/h) or Mach 1·2 at sea level, 1,450 mph (2 335 km/h) or Mach 2·2 at 39,370 ft (12 000 m); range cruise, 550 mph (885 km/h) at 29,530 ft (9 000 m); range with max. external fuel, 2,050 mls (3 300 km), with max. external combat load of 8,818 lb (4 000 kg), 560 mls (900 km), with external combat load of 4,410 lb (2 000 kg), 1,430 mls (2 300 km); service ceiling, 65,600 ft (20 000 m).

Weights: Empty, 16,314 lb (7 400 kg); loaded (clean), 24,030 lb (10 900 kg); max. take-off, 32,850 lb (14 900 kg).

Armament: Two 30-mm DEFA cannon and (intercept) 1-3 Matra 530 and two AIM-9 Sidewinder AAMs, or (attack) eight 882-lb (400-kg) bombs, six 66 imp gal (300·l) napalm tanks, five 18-rocket pods, or mix of bombs and missiles, the latter including the AS.30 and AS.37 Martel ASMs.

Status: First of four prototypes flown December 23, 1966. Eighty-five ordered for *Armée de l'Air* by beginning of 1972 with deliveries scheduled to commence in July 1973. Licence manufacture is to be undertaken in South Africa.

Notes: Initial model for *Armée de l'Air* intended primarily for high-altitude intercept role. Proposed versions include F1A for day ground attack role, the F1B two-seat trainer, the F1C interceptor, the F1E multi-role version, and the F1R reconnaissance model. Later models are to receive the SNECMA M53 turbojet with a reheat thrust of approximately 18,740 lb (8 500 kg). An M53-powered Mirage F1 is to fly in 1974.

DASSAULT/BREGUET MIRAGE F1

Dimensions: Span, 27 ft $6\frac{1}{4}$ in (8,40 m); length, 49 ft $2\frac{1}{2}$ in (15,00 m); height, 14 ft 9 in (4,50 m); wing area, 269·098 sq ft (25 m²).

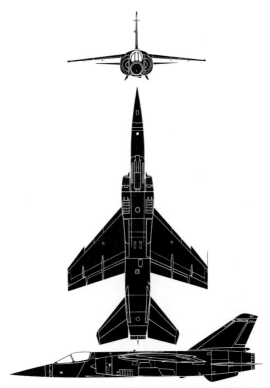

DASSAULT/BREGUET MIRAGE G8

Country of Origin: France.
Type: Experimental two-seat multi-purpose fighter.
Power Plant: Two 15,873 lb (7 200 kg) reheat SNECMA Atar 9K-50 turbojets.
Performance: (Estimated) Max. speed, 990 mph (1 590 km/h) or Mach 1·3 at sea level, 1,650 mph (2 655 km/h) or Mach 2·5 at 41,000 ft (12 500 m).
Weights: Approx. max. take-off, 44,090 lb (20 000 kg).
Status: First of two Mirage G8 prototypes flown on May 8, 1971, and second prototype scheduled to fly during course of 1972.
Notes: The Mirage G8, which is eventually to be re-engined with advanced-technology SNECMA M53 engines of 18,650 lb (8 460 kg) thrust with reheat, has been derived from the single-engined Mirage G1 (see 1971 edition) which was destroyed in an accident on January 13, 1971. It is serving as a basis for a variable-geometry multi-purpose fighter proposed for *Armée de l'Air* service from 1978–79, fulfilling the roles of patrol, attack and long-range reconnaissance. The Mirage G8 is equipped with the multi-mode Thomson-CSF Cyrano IV radar, a low-altitude navigational-attack system based on that of the Jaguar and including laser range-finding, doppler and bombing computer elements. The wings are swept 23 deg in the furthest forward position and approximately 70 deg in the furthest aft position. No production funding for a derivative of the Mirage G8 is included in the current (1971–76) defence budget.

DASSAULT/BREGUET MIRAGE G8

Dimensions: *No details available for publication.*

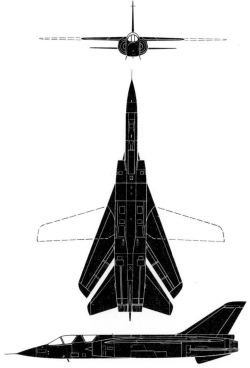

DE HAVILLAND CANADA DHC-5 BUFFALO

Country of Origin: Canada.

Type: STOL military utility transport.

Power Plant: Two 3,055 eshp General Electric CT64-820-1 turboprops.

Performance: Max. cruise, 282 mph (454 km/h) at 10,000 ft (3 050 m); cruise at 80% power, 253 mph (407 km/h), at 52% power, 208 mph (335 km/h); range with 14,100-lb (6 395-kg) payload, 518 mls (834 km), with 8,000-lb (3 629-kg) payload, 1,600 mls (2 575 km), with zero payload, 2,220 mls (3 572 kg); initial climb, 2,080 ft/min (10,56 m/sec); service ceiling, 31,500 ft (9 600 m).

Weights: Operational empty, 22,900 lb (10 387 kg); design take-off, 41,000 lb (18 597 kg); max. overload, 45,100 lb (20 457 kg).

Accommodation: Flight crew of three and 41 troops, 35 paratroops, or 24 casualty stretchers and six medical attendants or seated casualties.

Status: First of four evaluation aircraft (C-8A) for US Army flown April 9, 1964. Deliveries against initial order for 15 (CC-115) for Canadian Armed Forces commenced 1967, 24 delivered to Brazilian Air Force 1969–70, and delivery of 16 for Peruvian Air Force commenced in 1971.

Notes: Development costs shared equally between the US Army, the Canadian Government and de Havilland Canada.

DE HAVILLAND CANADA DHC-5 BUFFALO

Dimensions: Span, 99 ft 0 in (29,26 m); length, 79 ft 0 in (24,08 m); height, 28 ft 8 in (8,73 m); wing area, 945 sq ft (87,8 m²).

DE HAVILLAND CANADA DHC-6
TWIN OTTER SERIES 300

Country of Origin: Canada.
Type: STOL utility transport and feederliner.
Power Plant: Two 652 eshp Pratt & Whitney PT6A-27 turboprops.
Performance: Max. cruise, 210 mph (338 km/h) at 10,000 ft (3 050 m); range at max. cruise with 3,250-lb (1 474-kg) payload, 745 mls (1 198 km), with 14 passengers and 45 min reserves, 780 mls (1 255 km); initial climb at 12,500 lb (5 670 kg), 1,600 ft/min (8,1 m/sec); service ceiling, 26,700 ft (8 138 m).
Weights: Basic operational (including pilot), 7,000 lb (3 180 kg); max. take-off, 12,500 lb (5 670 kg).
Accommodation: Flight crew of one or two and accommodation for up to 20 passengers in basic commuter arrangement. Optional commuter layouts for 18 or 19 passengers, and 13–20-passenger utility version.
Status: First of five (Series 100) pre-production aircraft flown May 20, 1965. Series 100 superseded by Series 200 (see 1969 edition) in April 1968, the latter joined by the Series 300 with the 231st aircraft off the assembly line, deliveries of this version commencing spring 1969.
Notes: Series 100 and 200 Twin Otters have 579 eshp PT6A-20s, and the Twin Otter is available as a floatplane.

DHC-6 TWIN OTTER SERIES 300

Dimensions: Span, 65 ft 0 in (19,81 m); length, 51 ft 9 in (15,77 m); height, 18 ft 7 in (5,66 m); wing area, 420 sq ft (39,02 m²).

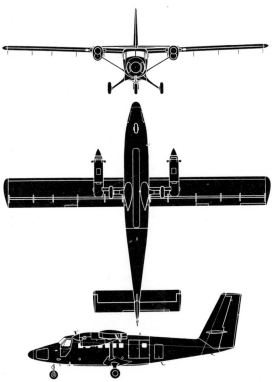

DORNIER DO 28D-2 SKYSERVANT

Country of Origin: Federal Germany.

Type: Light STOL utility aircraft.

Power Plant: Two 380 hp Lycoming IGSO-540-A1E six-cylinder horizontally-opposed engines.

Performance: Max. speed, 199 mph (320 km/h) at 10,000 ft (3 050 m); max. cruise at 75% power, 178 mph (286 km/h) at 10,000 ft (3 050 m); econ. cruise, 143 mph (230 km/h); range with max. fuel and without reserves at econ. cruise, 1,143 mls (1 837 km); initial climb, 1,180 ft/min (6 m/sec); service ceiling, 24,280 ft (7 400 m).

Weights: Empty, 4,775 lb (2 166 kg); max. take-off, 8,050 lb (3 650 kg).

Accommodation: Flight crew of one or two, and 12 passengers in individual seats in main cabin, 13 passengers in inward-facing folding seats, or (ambulance role) five casualty stretchers and five seats for medical attendants or sitting casualties.

Status: First of three prototype Do 28Ds flown February 23, 1966, with production deliveries commencing summer 1967. Production rate of six—eight per month at beginning of 1972.

Notes: Total of 125 Do 28Ds in process of delivery to *Luftwaffe* (105) and *Marineflieger* (20), four of those for the former service are used by the VIP transport unit, the *Flugbereitschaft*. The Skyservant may be fitted with wheel-ski gear or floats.

DORNIER DO 28D-2 SKYSERVANT

Dimensions: Span, 50 ft 10¾ in (15,50 m); length, 37 ft 4¾ in (11,40 m); height, 12 ft 9½ in (3,90 m); wing area, 308 sq ft (28,6 m²).

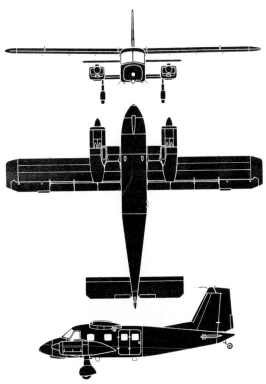

FAIRCHILD YA-10A

Country of Origin: USA.

Type: Single-seat close-support and attack aircraft.

Power Plant: Two (approx.) 9,000 lb (4 080 kg) General Electric TF34 turbofans.

Performance: (Estimated) Max. speed in excess of 460 mph (740 km/h); endurance with 16,000 lb (7 257 kg) of external ordnance, up to 4 hrs.

Weights: (Estimated) Operational empty, 21,300 lb (9 661 kg); max. take-off, 45,825 lb (20 786 kg).

Armament: One 30-mm cannon with 1,350 rounds and max. external ordnance load of 16,000 lb (7 257 kg). Typical external loads to comprise 24 500-lb (227-kg) Mk 82 bombs, 16 750-lb (340-kg) Mk 117 bombs, four 2,000-lb (907-kg) Mk 84 bombs, 20 Rockeye II cluster bombs, or nine AGM-65 Maverick ASMs.

Status: Two YA-10As ordered December 1970 for competitive evaluation with Northrop YA-9A (see page 180), both YA-10As being scheduled to commence flight testing in June 1972. Anticipated USAF orders for total of 600 of selected aircraft.

Notes: The YA-10A has been designed to meet the requirements of the USAF's A-X (Attack-Experimental) specification, primary objectives of the programme being low cost, and high effectiveness and survivability. It is to operate from short battlefield-area airstrips, taking-off within 1,000 ft (305 m) with a reasonable payload. A 12-month USAF evaluation is expected to commence in November 1972.

FAIRCHILD YA-10A

Dimensions: Span, 54 ft 8 in (16,66 m); length, 54 ft 8 in (16,66 m); height, 15 ft 5 in (4,70 m); wing area, 600 sq ft (55,74 m²).

FMA IA 58 PUCARÁ

Country of Origin: Argentina.

Type: Tandem two-seat counter-insurgency aircraft.

Power Plant: Two 1,022 eshp Turboméca Astazou XVIG turboprops.

Performance: Max. speed, 323 mph (520 km/h) at 9,840 ft (3 000 m); max. cruise, 301 mph (485 km/h) at 9,840 ft (3 000 m); econ. cruise, 267 mph (430 km/h); range with two 66 Imp gal (300 l) auxiliary tanks, 1,890 mls (3 040 km) at 16,400 ft (5 000 m); initial climb rate, 3,543 ft/min (18,0 m/sec); service ceiling, 27,165 ft (8 280 m).

Weights: (With TPE-331-U-303 turboprops) Empty equipped, 7,826 lb (3 550 kg); max. take-off, 13,668 lb (6 200 kg).

Armament: Two 20-mm Hispano cannon and four 7,62-mm FN machine guns. One hard point beneath fuselage and one beneath each wing for various combinations of bombs, missiles or weapons pods.

Status: First prototype flown on August 20, 1969, and second prototype on September 6, 1970. Preparations for an initial production batch of 50 aircraft initiated late 1971.

Notes: First prototype (see 1971 edition) powered by two 904 ehp Garrett AirResearch TPE-331-U-303 turboprops, but second prototype (illustrated) and production aircraft have the Astazou XVIG which has been standardised. The Pucará has been designed specifically to meet the requirements of the Argentine Air Force which reportedly possesses a requirement for a total of 80 aircraft of this type, and the first production deliveries of the Pucará to that service are expected to be made before the end of 1973.

FMA IA 58 PUCARÁ

Dimensions: Span, 47 ft 6¾ in (14,50 m); length, 45 ft 7¼ in (13,90 m); height, 17 ft 2¼ in (5,24 m); wing area, 326·1 sq ft (30,3 m²).

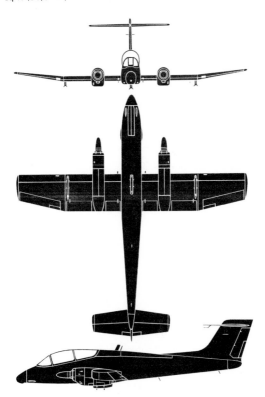

FOKKER F.27 FRIENDSHIP SRS. 500

Country of Origin: Netherlands.

Type: Short- to medium-range commercial transport.

Power Plant: Two 2,250 eshp Rolls-Royce Dart 532-7 turboprops.

Performance: Max. cruise, 322 mph (518 km/h) at 20,000 ft (6 095 m); normal cruise at 38,000 lb (17 237 kg), 292 mph (470 km/h) at 20,000 ft (6 095 m); range with max. payload, 667 mls (1 075 km), with max. fuel and 9,680-lb (4 390-kg) payload, 1,099 mls (1 805 km); initial climb at max. take-off weight, 1,200 ft/min (6,1 m/sec); service ceiling at 38,000 lb (17 237 kg), 28,500 ft (8 690 m).

Weights: Empty, 25,300 lb (11 475 kg); operational empty, 26,190 lb (11 879 kg); max. take-off, 45,000 lb (20 411 kg).

Accommodation: Basic flight crew of two or three and standard seating for 52 passengers. Alternative arrangements for up to 56 passengers.

Status: First Srs. 500 flown November 15, 1967. Production currently standardising on Srs. 500 and 600. Orders for the Friendship (including those licence-built in the USA by Fairchild) totalled 580 by beginning of 1972.

Notes: By comparison with basic Srs. 200 (see 1968 edition), the Srs. 500 has a 4 ft 11 in (1,5 m) fuselage stretch. The Srs. 400 "Combiplane" (see 1966 edition) and the equivalent military Srs. 400M are convertible cargo or combined cargo-passenger versions of the Srs. 200, and the current Srs. 600 is similar to the Srs. 400 but lacks the reinforced and watertight cargo floor.

FOKKER F.27 FRIENDSHIP SRS. 500

Dimensions: Span, 95 ft $1\frac{3}{4}$ in (29,00 m); length, 82 ft $2\frac{1}{2}$ in (25,06 m); height, 28 ft $7\frac{1}{4}$ in (8,71 m); wing area, 753·47 sq ft (70 m²).

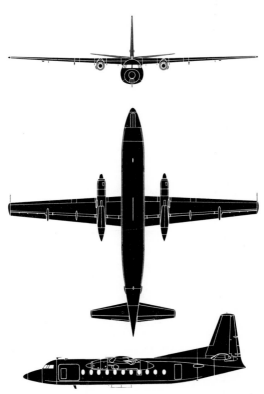

FOKKER F.28 FELLOWSHIP MK 2000

Country of Origin: Netherlands.

Type: Short-range commercial transport.

Power Plant: Two 9,850 lb (4 468 kg) Rolls-Royce RB.183-2 Spey Mk. 555-15 turbofans.

Performance: Max. cruise, 528 mph (849 km/h) at 21,000 ft (6 400 m); best-cost cruise, 508 mph (817 km/h) at 30,000 ft (9 150 m); long-range cruise, 423 mph (680 km/h) at 30,000 ft (9 150 m); range with 75 passengers, 846 mls (1 362 km), with max. fuel (standard tankage), 1,215 mls (1 955 km).

Weights: Operational empty, 36,310 lb (16 470 kg); max. take-off, 65,000 lb (29 485 kg).

Accommodation: Flight crew of two or three and 48 passengers four-abreast or 75–79 passengers five-abreast.

Status: Mk 2000 prototype flown on April 28, 1971, with first production model scheduled to fly mid-1972.

Notes: The Fellowship Mk 2000 is a stretched development of the Mk 1000 (see 1971 edition), additional fuselage sections permitting an increase in passenger accommodation. The prototype of the Mk 2000 (illustrated above) is actually a conversion of the first pre-production Mk 1000, the fuselage being lengthened by 7 ft 3 in (2,21 m) by the addition of 57 in (1,45 m) forward of the wing and 30 in (0,76 m) aft. Orders for the shorter-fuselage Mk 1000 stood at 50 aircraft at the beginning of 1972. The Fellowship is a European co-operative effort with components built by VFW-Fokker and MBB in Germany and Short Brothers in the UK.

FOKKER F.28 FELLOWSHIP MK 2000

Dimensions: Span, 77 ft 4¼ in (23,58 m); length, 97 ft 1¾ in (29,61 m); height, 27 ft 9½ in (8,47 m); wing area, 822 sq ft (76,4 m²).

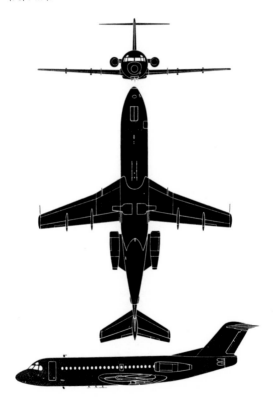

GAF N2

Country of Origin: Australia.

Type: STOL utility transport.

Power Plant: Two 400 shp Allison 250-B17 turboprops.

Performance: Max. speed, 212 mph (341 km/h) at sea level; max. cruise, 200 mph (322 km/h) at sea level; econ. cruise, 165 mph (266 km/h); range with max. fuel and 45 min reserves, 1,036 mls (1 665 km); initial climb, 1,800 ft/ min (9,14 m/sec); service ceiling, 27,500 ft (8 380 m).

Weights: Empty, 3,640 lb (1 651 kg); max. take-off, 7,700 lb (3 493 kg).

Accommodation: Basic flight crew of two and seating for a maximum of 13 passengers.

Status: Two prototypes flown July 23 and December 5, 1971, and proposed production versions include the military N22 and the commercial N24.

Notes: Developed by the Government Aircraft Factories as a multi-purpose military STOL aircraft suitable for operation in forward areas, the N2 incorporates ejection seats for the crew members, armour protection, and self-sealing fuel tanks, and while the primary roles foreseen for the military version are transport and liaison, the Australian Army has considered its suitability for the close-support, reconnaissance and forward air control missions. The proposed commercial development, the N24, features 5 ft (1,52 m) lengthening of the fuselage and will be offered with accommodation for seven to 15 passengers. The military N22 will have provision for two pylons beneath the outer wings and two beneath the roots of the stub wings for ordnance loads.

GAF N2

Dimensions: Span, 54 ft 0 in (16,46 m); length, 40 ft 10 in (12,45 m); height, 15 ft 11 in (4,85 m); wing area, 320 sq ft (29,7 m²).

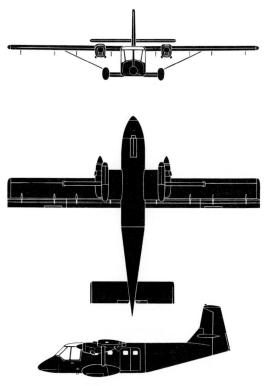

GRUMMAN A-6 INTRUDER

Country of Origin: USA.

Type: Two-seat shipboard low-level strike aircraft.

Power Plant: Two 9,300 lb (4 218 kg) Pratt & Whitney J52-P-8A turbojets.

Performance: Max. speed at 36,655 lb (16 626 kg) in clean condition, 685 mph (1 102 km/h) or Mach 0·9 at sea level, 625 mph (1 006 km/h) or Mach 0·94 at 36,000 ft (10 970 m); average cruise, 480 mph (772 km/h) at 32,750–43,800 ft (9 980–13 350 m); range with max. internal fuel and four Bullpup ASMs, 1,920 mls (3 090 km), with single store and four 250 Imp gal (1 136 l) external tanks, 3,040 mls (4 890 km).

Weights: Empty, 25,684 lb (11 650 kg); loaded (clean), 37,116 lb (16 836 kg); max. overload take-off, 60,280 lb (27 343 kg).

Armament: Max. external ordnance load of 15,000 lb (6 804 kg) distributed between five 3,600-lb (1 633-kg) stores stations.

Status: First of eight test and development aircraft flown April 19, 1960 and first delivery to US Navy (A-6A) on February 7, 1963.

Notes: Specification relates to basic A-6A (see 1970 edition), drawing depicts A-6B which differs in having equipment for AGM-78A Standard ARM (Anti-Radiation Missile), the A-6C has a detachable ventral turret for low-light television and infra-red sensors, and the KA-6D (illustrated above) is a shipboard tanker version. The A-6E has more advanced avionics and flew in prototype form on February 27, 1970. The EA-6A and EA-6B (see 1969 edition) are two- and four-seat electronic counter-measures versions respectively.

GRUMMAN A-6 INTRUDER

Dimensions: Span, 53 ft 0 in (16,15 m); length, 54 ft 7 in (16,64 m); height, 15 ft 7 in (4,75 m); wing area, 529 sq ft (49,15 m²).

103

GRUMMAN F-14A TOMCAT

Country of Origin: USA.

Type: Two-seat shipboard multi-purpose fighter.

Power Plant: Two (approx) 20,600 lb (9 344 kg) reheat Pratt & Whitney TF30-P-412 turbofans.

Performance: (Estimated) Max. speed with four AIM-7 Sparrow missiles for intercept mission at approx. 57,300 lb (25 990 kg), 910 mph (1 470 km/h) or Mach 1·2 at sea level, 1,564 mph (2 517 km/h) or Mach 2·34 at 40,000 ft (12 190 m).

Weights: (Estimated) Empty, 36,000 lb (16 330 kg); normal take-off (intercept mission), 57,300 lb (25 990 kg).

Armament: One 20-mm M-61A1 rotary cannon and (intercept mission) four AIM-7 Sparrow and four AIM-9 Sidewinder AAMs or six AIM-54 Phoenix and two AIM-9 AAMs.

Status: First of 12 research and development aircraft commenced flight trials on December 21, 1970, followed by second on May 24, 1971. US Navy anticipated total buy of 301 F-14 series fighters at beginning of 1972.

Notes: F-14A is scheduled to attain operational status in 1973, and it is anticipated that the 123rd and subsequent aircraft will be completed to F-14B standard with advanced technology Pratt & Whitney F401-PW-401 turbofans of some 30,000 lb (13 610 kg), increasing thrust/weight ratio from 0·84 to 1·16, estimated acceleration from Mach 0·8 to Mach 1·8 being 1·27 minutes. The F-14B is expected to commence fleet indoctrination late 1974 or early 1975. The proposed F-14C version of the Tomcat embodies a more advanced avionics system.

GRUMMAN F-14A TOMCAT

Dimensions: Span (max.), 64 ft 1½ in (19,54 m), (min.), 33 ft 2½ in (10,12 m); length, 61 ft 10½ in (18,86 m); height, 16 ft 0 in (4,88 m).

HAWKER SIDDELEY 125-600

Country of Origin: United Kingdom.
Type: Light business executive transport.
Power Plant: Two 3,750 lb (1 701 kg) Rolls-Royce Viper 601 turbojets.
Performance: (Estimated) Max. cruise, 510 mph (820 km/h) at 31,000 ft (9 450 m); econ. cruise, 450 mph (734 km/h) at 38,000 ft (11 580 m); range with max. fuel and reserves for 45 min hold, 1,960 mls (3 154 km); initial climb, 3,600 ft/min (18,3 m/sec); service ceiling, 41,000 ft (12 495 m).
Weights: (Estimated) Empty equipped, 12,500 lb (5 670 kg); max. take-off, 25,000 lb (7 620 kg).
Accommodation: Normal flight crew of two and alternative interior layouts for from six to 14 passengers.
Status: First of two prototype HS 125-600s was flown for the first time on January 21, 1971, and development was continuing at low key at the beginning of 1972.
Notes: The HS 125-600, which is to be marketed in North America by the Beech Aircraft Corporation as the BH-600, is essentially a higher-powered, stretched version of the HS 125-400 (see 1970 edition) which is marketed by Beech as the BH 125-400, an additional section in the forward fuselage permitting two more passengers to be accommodated, and the Viper 601s providing more thrust and improved specific fuel consumption. Production plans for the HS 125-600 had not been finalised at the time of closing for press when sales of the earlier versions of the HS 125 had attained 252 aircraft.

HAWKER SIDDELEY 125-600

Dimensions: Span, 47 ft 0 in (14,33 m); length, 50 ft 6 in (15,39 m); height, 17 ft 3 in (5,25 m); wing area, 353 sq ft (32,8 m²).

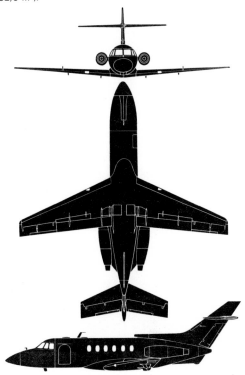

HAWKER SIDDELEY 748 SERIES 2A

Country of Origin: United Kingdom.

Type: Short- to medium-range commercial transport.

Power Plant: Two 2,280 ehp Rolls-Royce Dart R.Da.7 Mk. 532-2L turboprops.

Performance: Max. speed at 40,000 lb (18 145 kg), 312 mph (502 km/h) at 16,000 ft (4 875 m); max. cruise, 287 mph (462 km/h) at 15,000 ft (4 570 m); econ. cruise, 267 mph (430 km/h) at 20,000 ft (6 095 m); range cruise, 259 mph (418 km/h) at 25,000 ft (7 620 m); range with max. fuel and reserves for 45 min hold and 230-mile (370-km) diversion, 1,862 mls (2 996 km), with max. payload and same reserves, 690 mls (1 110 km).

Weights: Basic operational, 25,361 lb (11 504 kg); max. take-off, 44,495 lb (20 182 kg).

Accommodation: Normal flight crew of two and standard cabin arrangement for 40 passengers in paired seats. Alternative high-density arrangement for 58 passengers.

Status: First prototype flown June 24, 1960, and first production model (Srs. 1) on August 30, 1961. Srs. 1 superseded by Srs. 2 in 1962, this being in turn superseded by current Srs. 2A from mid-1967. Total of 258 ordered by beginning of 1972.

Notes: Manufactured under licence in India by HAL for Indian Airlines (24) and Indian Air Force (five Srs. 1 and 22 Srs. 2) at rate of nine per year.

HAWKER SIDDELEY 748 SERIES 2A

Dimensions: Span, 98 ft 6 in (30,02 m); length, 67 ft 0 in (20,42 m); height, 24 ft 10 in (7,57 m); wing area, 810·75 sq ft (75,35 m²).

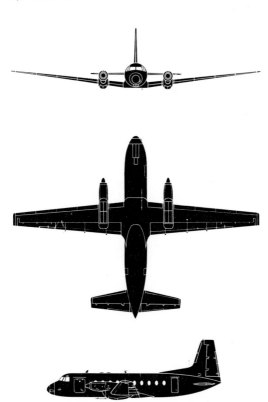

HAWKER SIDDELEY BUCCANEER
S. MK. 2B

Country of Origin: United Kingdom.

Type: Two-seat strike and reconnaissance aircraft.

Power Plant: Two 11,100 lb (5 035 kg) Rolls-Royce RB. 168-1A Spey Mk. 101 turbofans.

Performance: (Estimated) Max. speed, 645 mph (1 040 km/h) or Mach 0·85 at 250 ft (75 m), 620 mph (998 km/h) or Mach 0·92 at 30,000 ft (9 145 m); typical low-level cruise, 570 mph (917 km/h) or Mach 0·75 at 3,000 ft (915 m); tactical radius for hi-lo-lo-hi mission with standard fuel, 500—600 mls (805—965 km).

Weights: Max. take-off, 59,000 lb (26 762 kg).

Armament: Max. ordnance load of 16,000 lb (7 257 kg), including four 500-lb (227-kg), 540-lb (245-kg), or 1,000-lb (453,5-kg) bombs internally, and up to three 1,000-lb (453,5-kg) or six 500-lb (227-kg) bombs on each of four wing stations.

Status: First S. Mk. 2B for RAF flown January 8, 1970, with deliveries of 42 built to this standard continuing into 1973. Proportion of 84 S. Mk. 2s built for Royal Navy being modified for RAF use as S. Mk. 2As, and most of these ultimately to be converted to S. Mk. 2Bs.

Notes: The S. Mk. 2A embodies avionic, system, and equipment modifications for RAF service, and wing and weapon-pylon changes to provide Martel missile capability. S. Mk. 2B introduces 425 Imp gal (1 932 l) fuel tank on rotating bomb door (seen on accompanying drawing) and undercarriage changes to accommodate new gross weight of 59,000 lb (26 762 kg).

HAWKER SIDDELEY BUCCANEER S. MK. 2B

Dimensions: Span, 44 ft 0 in (13,41 m); length, 63 ft 5 in (19,33 m); height, 16 ft 3 in (4,95 m); wing area, 514·7 sq ft (47,82 m²).

HAWKER SIDDELEY HARRIER G.R. MK. 1

Country of Origin: United Kingdom.
Type: Single-seat V/STOL strike and reconnaissance fighter.
Power Plant: One 19,200 lb (8 710 kg) Rolls-Royce Bristol Pegasus 101 vectored-thrust turbofan.
Performance: Max. speed, 720 mph (1 160 km/h) or Mach 0·95 at 1,000 ft (305 m), with typical external ordnance load, 640–660 mph (1 030–1 060 km) or Mach 0·85–0·87 at 1,000 ft (305 m); max. speed in clean condition at 35,000 ft (10 670 m), 610 mph (980 km/h) or Mach 0·93; tactical radius for hi-lo-hi mission with two 100 Imp gal (455 l) external tanks, 400 mls (644 km); ferry range with two 330 Imp gal (1 500 l) external tanks, 2,250 mls (3 620 km).
Weights: Empty equipped, 13,550 lb (6 146 kg); max. take-off (VTOL), 16,000 lb (7 257 kg); max. take-off (STOL), 21,500 lb (9 752 kg).
Armament: Provision for two 30-mm Aden cannon with 130 rpg and up to 5,000 lb (2 268 kg) of ordnance on five external stores stations.
Status: First of six pre-production aircraft flown August 31, and first production G.R. Mk. 1 following on December 28, 1967. Current orders for RAF call for 77 G.R. Mk. 1s plus 13 two-seat T. Mk. 2s (see 1969 edition). First T. Mk. 2 development aircraft flown April 24, 1969, and first Mk. 50 for the US Marine Corps flown November 20, 1970.
Notes: Export models with 21,500 lb (9 752 kg) Pegasus 103 known as Mk. 50 (single-seat) and Mk. 51 (two-seat). Initial batch of 30 Mk. 50s for US Marine Corps (as AV-8As) for delivery completion in 1972, first 10 delivered in 1971 with interim 20,500-lb (9 300-kg) Pegasus 102. Further 84 planned for delivery to the USMC during 1972–75.

112

HAWKER SIDDELEY HARRIER G.R. MK. 1

Dimensions: Span, 25 ft 3 in (7,70 m); length, 45 ft 7¾ in (13,91 m); height, 11 ft 3 in (3,43 m); wing area, 201·1 sq ft (18,68 m²).

HAWKER SIDDELEY NIMROD M.R. MK. 1

Country of Origin: United Kingdom.

Type: Long-range maritime patrol aircraft.

Power Plant: Four (approx) 11,500 lb (5 217 kg) Rolls-Royce RB. 168-20 Spey Mk. 250 turbofans.

Performance: (Estimated) Max. cruise, 500–530 mph (805-853 km/h) at 31,000–33,000 ft (9 450–10 060 m); long-range cruise, 460 mph (740 km/h) at 30,000 ft (9 145 m); minimum search speed, 210 mph (338 km/h); loiter endurance on two engines, 12–14 hrs.

Weights: Max. take-off 175,000–178,000 lb (79 380–80 740 kg).

Armament: Ventral weapons bay accommodating full range of ASW weapons (homing torpedoes, mines, depth charges, etc) and two underwing pylons for AS.12 or Martel ASMs.

Accommodation: Normal flight crew of three on flight deck with nine navigators and sensor operators in tactical compartment. Provision is made for conversion for the trooping role and in this configuration up to 45 troops may be accommodated in the rear pressure cabin.

Status: First of two Nimrod prototypes employing modified Comet 4C airframes flown May 23, 1967. First of initial batch of 38 production Nimrod M.R. Mk. 1s flown on June 28, 1968, followed by first delivery to RAF on October 2, 1969. M.R. Mk. 1s followed by three Nimrod R. Mk. 1s for special reconnaissance duties. Initial RAF order completed 1971, but it was anticipated early 1972 that a supplementary contract would be placed during the course of the year.

Notes: The world's first shore-based turbojet-propelled maritime patrol aircraft, the Nimrod employs the basic structure of the Comet 4C transport (see 1963 edition) and is equipping five RAF squadrons.

114

HAWKER SIDDELEY NIMROD M.R. MK. 1

Dimensions: Span, 114 ft 10 in (35,00 m); length, 126 ft 9 in (38,63 m); height, 29 ft $8\frac{1}{2}$ in (9,01 m); wing area, 2,121 sq ft (197,05 m²).

HAWKER SIDDELEY TRIDENT 3B

Country of Origin: United Kingdom.

Type: Short-haul commercial transport.

Power Plant: Three 11,930 lb (5 411 kg) Rolls-Royce RB.163–25 Mk. 512-5W turbofans plus one 5,250 lb (2 381 kg) Rolls-Royce RB.162-86 turbojet.

Performance: Max. cruise, 601 mph (967 km/h) at 28,300 ft (8 625 m); econ. cruise, 533 mph (858 km/h) at 29,000–33,000 ft (8 000–10 000 m); typical high-speed cruise, 580 mph (933 km/h) at 25,000 ft (7 620 m); range with max. payload and reserves for 250 mls (402 km) and 45 min hold, 1,658 mls (2 668 km), with max. payload and same reserves, 1,094 mls (1 760 km).

Weights: Operational empty as 128-seater, 83,473 lb (37 863 kg), as 152-seater, 83,104 lb (37 695 kg); max. take-off, 150,000 lb (68 040 kg).

Accommodation: Basic flight crew of three and alternative arrangements for 14 first-class and 114 tourist-class passengers, or 152 tourist-class passengers. High-density arrangements for 164 or 171 passengers.

Status: First Trident 3B flown December 11, 1969. Twenty-six (with options on 10 more) ordered for BEA, with which airline the Trident 3B entered service on April 1, 1971.

Notes: The Trident 3B is a high-capacity short-haul development of the Trident 1E (see 1966 edition) with a stretched fuselage and similar power plants and wing modifications to those of the Trident 2E (see 1969 edition). The 3B also embodies wing area, wing incidence, and flap span increases, and an RB.162-86 auxiliary turbojet in the tail to boost take-off and climb-out.

HAWKER SIDDELEY TRIDENT 3B

Dimensions: Span, 98 ft 0 in (29,87 m); length, 131 ft 2 in (39,98 m); height, 28 ft 3 in (8,61 m); wing area, 1,493 sq ft (138,7 m²).

HISPANO HA-220 SUPER SAETA

Country of Origin: Spain.
Type: Single-seat light ground attack aircraft.
Power Plant: Two 1,058 lb (480 kg) Turboméca Marboré VI turbojets.
Performance: Max. speed, 410 mph (660 km/h) or Mach 0·54 at sea level, 430 mph (692 km/h) or Mach 0·63 at 22,965 ft (7 000 m); max. cruise, 340 mph (547 km/h) at sea level, 360 mph (580 km/h) at 19,685 ft (6 000 m); range with max. internal fuel and no reserves, 510 mls (820 km) at sea level, 1,025 mls (1 650 km) at 29,530 ft (9 000 m); service ceiling, 42,650 ft (13 000 m).
Weights: (Estimated) Empty equipped, 4,630 lb (2 100 kg); max. take-off, 7,937 lb (3 600 kg).
Armament: Two 7,7-mm Breda machine guns and various ordnance loads on four 551-lb (250-kg) capacity wing and two 375-lb (170-kg) capacity fuselage stores stations.
Status: First of initial batch of 25 HA-220s ordered for Spanish Air Force flown on April 25, 1970.
Notes: The HA-220 is a single-seat ground attack derivative of the HA-200E Super Saeta advanced trainer (see 1969 edition) from which it differs primarily in having self-sealing fuel tanks, an additional tank in place of the second seat of the trainer, light armour protection, additional stores stations, and appropriate avionics.

118

HISPANO HA-220 SUPER SAETA

Dimensions: Span, 34 ft 2 in (10,42 m), over tip-tanks, 35 ft 10 in (10,93 m); length, 29 ft 5 in (8,97 m); height, 9 ft 4 in (2,85 m); wing area, 187·2 sq ft (17,4 m²).

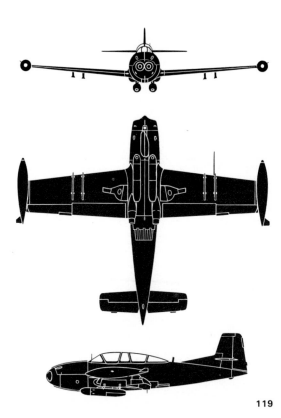

119

IAI-101 ARAVA

Country of Origin: Israel.
Type: Light STOL general-purpose transport.
Power Plant: Two 715 eshp Pratt & Whitney PT6A-27 turboprops.
Performance: Max. speed, 217 mph (350 km/h) at 10,000 ft (3 050 m); max. cruise, 197 mph (318 km/h) at 10,000 ft (3 050 m); range with max. fuel and 1,774-lb (805-kg) payload plus 30 min reserves, 867 mls (1 395 km), with max. payload and same reserves, 301 mls (486 km); initial climb, 1,715 ft/min (8,7 m/sec); service ceiling, 28,550 ft (8 700 m).
Weights: Empty equipped (utility), 7,343 lb (3 330 kg), (commuter), 7,790 lb (3 533 kg); max. take-off, 12,500 lb (5 670 kg).
Accommodation: Flight crew of one or two, and (commuter version) up to 20 passengers in four-abreast rows. Aeromedical layout for 12 casualty stretchers and medical attendants.
Status: First of four prototypes flown on November 27, 1969. Six pre-production examples to be completed during 1972 when production deliveries are scheduled to attain one per month, increasing to four per month in 1973.
Notes: Stretched version of the Arava accommodating up to 32 passengers currently envisaged with PT6A-40 turboprops, the military Arava 201 having PT6A-29 turboprops.

120

IAI-101 ARAVA

Dimensions: Span, 69 ft 6 in (20,88 m); length, 42 ft 7½ in (12,99 m); height, 17 ft 0¾ in (5,20 m); wing area, 470·2 sq ft (43,68 m²).

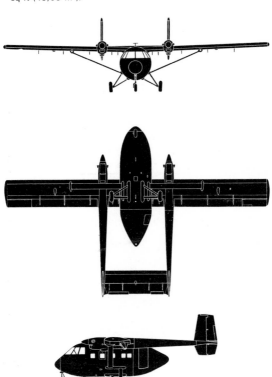

IAI COMMODORE JET ELEVEN23

Country of Origin: Israel.
Type: Light business executive transport.
Power Plant: Two 3,100 lb (1 406 kg) General Electric CJ610-9 turbojets.
Performance: Max. speed, 541 mph (871 km/h) at 19,500 ft (5 944 m); econ. cruise, 420 mph (676 km/h) at 41,000 ft (12 500 m); range with max. fuel and 45 min reserves, 2,120 mls (3 410 km), with 2,200-lb (998-kg) payload and same reserves, 1,600 mls (2 575 km); max. initial climb, 4,100 ft/min (20,83 m/sec); service ceiling, 45,000 ft (13 715 m).
Weights: Basic operational, 11,070 lb (5 021 kg); max. take-off, 20,800 lb (9 434 kg).
Accommodation: Normal flight crew of two and maximum of 10 passengers.
Status: First prototype (modified Jet Commander 1121) flown January 1970, and definitive prototype flown September 28, 1970. First production Commodore Jet Eleven23 flew early 1971 with first production deliveries commencing late in the same year.
Notes: Commodore Jet Eleven23 is derivative of Aero Commander Jet Commander 1121 (see 1966 edition) of which 149 built in USA. Tooling and jigs transferred to Israel where fuselage extended 22 in (55 cm), double-slotted Fowler-type flaps, wing leading-edge droop, lift dumpers, permanent wingtip tanks, more powerful turbojet, and other modifications have been introduced.

IAI COMMODORE JET ELEVEN23

Dimensions: Span, 44 ft 9½ in (13,65 m); length, 52 ft 3 in (15,92 m); height, 15 ft 9½ in (4,81 m); wing area, 303·3 sq ft (28,18 m²).

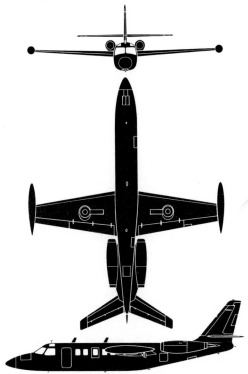

ILYUSHIN IL-62M-200 (CLASSIC)

Country of Origin: USSR.

Type: Long-range commercial transport.

Power Plant: Four 25,350 lb (11 500 kg) Soloviev D-30-KU turbofans.

Performance: Max. cruise, 560 mph (900 km/h) at 39,400 ft (12 000 m); range cruise, 528 mph (850 km/h) at 36,090 ft (11 000 m); range with max. payload and reserves, 4,970 mls (8 000 km), with max. fuel, 6,400 mls (10 300 km).

Weights: Max. take-off, 363,760 lb (165 000 kg).

Accommodation: Normal flight crew of five, and alternative configurations for 198 economy class, 186 tourist class or 161 mixed class passengers.

Status: First of two prototypes of the Il-62 flown January 1963, these being followed by three pre-production aircraft. Deliveries of basic Il-62 (to Aeroflot) began 1967, and developed Il-62M-200 scheduled to enter service early 1972.

Notes: The Il-62M-200, which appeared in 1971, differs from the basic Il-62 in having the 23,150 lb (10 500 kg) Kuznetsov NK-8-4 turbofans replaced by D-30-KU engines, and a small increase in passenger capacity achieved by re-arrangement of the toilet and wardrobe areas at the rear of the cabin. Other changes include the provision of a containerised baggage and freight system with mechanised loading and unloading, clam-shell thrust reversers on the outboard engines, and an additional fuel tank in the tailfin of 1,100 Imp gal (5 000 l) capacity. The flight deck has been revised and new communications and navigational equipment introduced.

ILYUSHIN IL-62M-200 (CLASSIC)

Dimensions: Span, 139 ft 5¼ in (42,50 m); length, 174 ft 2½ in (53,12 m); height, 40 ft 6¼ in (12,35 m); wing area, 3,008·5 sq ft (279,5 m²).

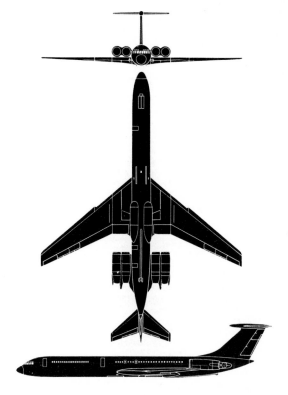

ILYUSHIN IL-38 (MAY)

Country of Origin: USSR.

Type: Long-range maritime patrol aircraft.

Power Plant: Four 4,250 ehp Ivchenko AI-20M turboprops.

Performance: (Estimated) Max. cruise, 400 mph (645 km/h) at 15,000 ft (4 570 m); normal cruise, 370 mph (395 km/h) at 26,250 ft (8 000 m); patrol speed, 250 mph (400 km/h) at 2,000 ft (610 m); max. range, 4,500 mls (7 240 km); loiter endurance, 12 hrs at 2,000 ft (610 m).

Weights: (Estimated) Empty equipped, 80,000 lb (36 287 kg); max. take-off, 140,000 lb (63 500 kg).

Accommodation: Normal flight crew believed to consist of 12 members of which half are housed in a tactical compartment.

Armament: Internal weapons bay for depth bombs. Wing hard points for external ordnance loads.

Status: A derivative of the Il-18 commercial transport (see 1966 edition), the Il-38 reportedly flew in prototype form in 1968 and entered service with the Soviet Naval Air Force in 1970.

Notes: The Il-38 maritime patrol aircraft has been evolved from the Il-18 transport in much the same fashion as the Lockheed P-3 Orion was developed from the Electra, the wings, engines, tail assembly and undercarriage of the Il-18 being married to a new fuselage embodying extensive ASW equipment, a tactical operations compartment and a weapons bay, and terminating in a MAD (Magnetic Anomaly Detection) tail 'sting'. The wing assembly is positioned further forward on the fuselage than on the commercial transport for CG reasons, and the Il-38 was reported during the course of 1971 in service with Soviet units based in Egypt and was also encountered by NATO forces in more northerly areas.

ILYUSHIN IL-38 (MAY)

Dimensions: Span, 122 ft 8½ in (37,40 m); length, 134 ft
0 in (40,83 m); height, 33 ft 4 in (10,17 m); wing area,
1,507 sq ft (140 m²).

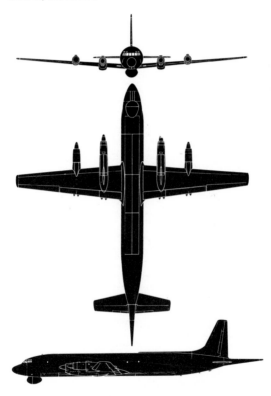

ILYUSHIN IL-76 (CANDID)

Country of Origin: USSR.

Type: Heavy commercial and military freighter.

Power Plant: Four 26,455 lb (12 000 kg) Soloviev D-30-KP turbofans.

Performance: Max. cruise, 528 mph (850 km/h) at 42,650 ft (13 000 m); range with max. payload, 3,107 mls (5 000 km).

Weights: Max. take-off, 346,122 lb (157 000 kg).

Accommodation: Normal flight crew of three–four on flight deck and in glazed nose, and pressurised hold for freight.

Status: Prototype flown for the first time on March 25, 1971, with production deliveries likely to commence in 1973–74.

Notes: Apparently evolved primarily to meet a military requirement, the Il-76 is generally similar in concept to the Lockheed C-141A StarLifter, but is slightly larger, more powerful and heavier. It employs a mechanised cargo-handling system, a high-flotation undercarriage, the main members of which comprise four individual units each of four parallel-mounted wheels, and extensive high-lift devices to achieve short-field performance. According to an official Soviet statement, the Il-76 is intended to operate from short unprepared strips in Siberia and other undeveloped areas of the Soviet Union during the period of the current five-year programme (1971–75). Clam-shell thrust reversers are fitted to all four power plants.

128

ILYUSHIN IL-76 (CANDID)

Dimensions: Span, 165 ft 8⅓ in (50,50 m); length, 152 ft 10¼ in (46,59 m); height, 48 ft 5⅝ in (14,76 m).

INTERCEPTOR 400

Country of Origin: USA.
Type: Light cabin monoplane.
Power Plant: One 400 shp Garrett-AiResearch TPE 331-1-101 turboprop.
Performance: Max. speed, 287 mph (463 km/h) at 16,000 ft (4 875 m); max. cruise, 281 mph (452 km/h) at 16,000 ft (4 875 m); econ. cruise, 281 mph (452 km/h); range, 1,000 mls (1 609 km); initial climb, 1,500 ft/min (7,62 m/sec).
Weights: Empty equipped, 2,300 lb (1 043 kg); max. take-off, 4,005 lb (1 816 kg).
Accommodation: Four seats in pairs in pressurised cabin.
Status: Prototype flown on June 27, 1969, and FAA certification acquired August 20, 1971, customer deliveries commencing November 1971. Production of one per month scheduled for 1972.
Notes: The Interceptor 400, which is claimed to be the first turboprop-powered, pressurised light cabin monoplane to be placed on the market, is a derivative of the piston-engined Meyers 200B which was subsequently produced as the Aero Commander 200 (see 1966 edition), all production jigs and tools for the latter having been acquired by the Interceptor Corporation. The TPE 331-1-101 turboprop of 665 shp is flat-rated at 400 shp, and pressurisation is relatively low, providing a cabin differential of 9,500 ft (2 895 m) at 18,000 ft (5 486 m) and 12,500 ft (3 810 m) at 22,000 ft (6 706 m).

INTERCEPTOR 400

Dimensions: Span, 30 ft 6 in (9,29 m); length, 26 ft 11¼ in (8,22 m); height, 8 ft 6 in (2,60 m); wing area, 161·5 sq ft (16,00 m²).

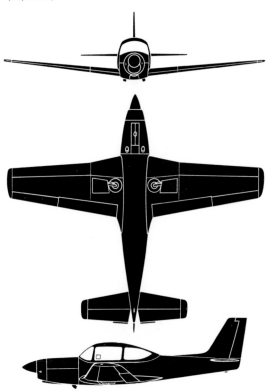

JETSTREAM SERIES 200

Country of Origin: United Kingdom.

Type: Light business executive and utility transport.

Power Plant: Two 940 eshp Turboméca Astazou XVI turbo-props.

Performance: Max. cruise, 285 mph (459 km/h) at 12,000 ft (3 660 m); range with max. fuel and 5% reserves plus 45 min hold, 1,382 mls (2 224 km); initial climb, 2,500 ft/min (12,7 m/sec).

Weights: Empty equipped (executive), 9,286 lb (4 212 kg); max. take-off, 12,500 lb (5 670 kg).

Accommodation: Normal flight crew of two and 12 passengers in executive layout with alternative 12–18 passenger commuter arrangements.

Status: Development initiated by Handley Page as the Jetstream 2, and flight testing resumed by Jetstream Aircraft Limited as the Jetstream Series 200 in December 1970. Initial batch of 20 aircraft under construction in 1971.

Notes: Jetstream Aircraft was formed to take over the development, production and marketing of the HP 137 Jetstream following the demise of the Handley Page company. The initial Handley Page-built version was the Jetstream 1 with Astazou XIV engines, 36 production examples of which were completed. Development of the Astazou XVI-powered Jetstream 2 was initiated by Handley Page with the re-engined first pre-production aircraft. Jetstream aircraft operates in collaboration with Scottish Aviation (manufacturer of the wing units for new production aircraft) in providing technical support for all Jetstream aircraft in service.

JETSTREAM SERIES 200

Dimensions: Span, 52 ft 0 in (15,85 m); length, 47 ft 1½ in (14,37 m); height, 17 ft 5½ in (5,32 m); wing area, 270 sq ft (25,08 m²).

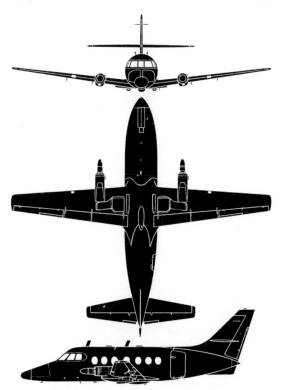

KAWASAKI XC-1A

Country of Origin: Japan.

Type: Medium-range military transport.

Power Plant: Two 14,500 lb (6 575 kg) Pratt & Whitney JT8D-9 turbofans.

Performance: (Estimated) Max. speed, 507 mph (815 km/h) at 23,200 ft (7 600 m); max. cruise, 438 mph (704 km/h) at 35,100 ft (10 700 m); range with max. fuel, 2,073 mls (3 335 km), with (normal) 17,637-lb (8 000-kg) payload, 806 mls (1 297 km); initial climb, 3,806 ft/min (19,3 m/sec); service ceiling, 39,370 ft (12 000 m).

Weights: Empty equipped, 50,706 lb (23 000 kg); max. take-off, 85,980 lb (39 000 kg).

Accommodation: Basic crew of five. Loads include 60 troops, 45 paratroops, or 36 casualty stretchers plus medical attendants. Cargo loads may include a 5,000-lb (2 268-kg) truck, a 105-mm howitzer, two 1,500-lb (680-kg) trucks, or three jeep-type vehicles.

Status: First of two flying prototypes flown on November 12, 1970, and second on January 16, 1971. Production deliveries scheduled to commence during the 1973 fiscal year, production attaining one per month during 1974.

Notes: The C-1A is intended as a successor to the aged Curtiss C-46 in Air Self-Defence Force squadrons, the service having a requirement for 38 aircraft.

134

KAWASAKI XC-1A

Dimensions: Span, 101 ft 8½ in (31,00 m); length, 95 ft 1¼ in (29,00 m); height, 32 ft 9¾ in (10,00 m); wing area, 1,291·7 sq ft (120 m²).

LET L 410 TURBOLET

Country of Origin: Czechoslovakia.
Type: Light utility transport and feederliner.
Power Plant: Two 715 eshp Pratt & Whitney PT6A-27 turboprops.
Performance: Max. cruise, 229 mph (370 km/h) at 9,840 ft (3 000 m); econ. cruise, 205 mph (330 km/h) at 9,840 ft (3 000 m); range with max. fuel and 45 min reserves, 705 mls (1 140 km), with max. payload and same reserves, 115 mls (185 km); initial climb rate, 1,595 ft/min (8,1 m/sec); service ceiling, 25,490 ft (7 770 m).
Weights: Empty equipped, 6,180 lb (2 803 kg); max. take-off, 11,245 lb (5 100 kg).
Accommodation: Basic flight crew of two. Configurations for 12, 15, 19 or 20 passengers in rows of three with two seats to starboard and one to port of aisle. Business executive layout available with accommodation for eight passengers.
Status: First of four prototypes flown April 16, 1969. Pre-production series of six aircraft built during 1971 of which two entered service with Slovak Air in September of that year. First production deliveries (to CSA) to commence in 1972.
Notes: Principal production version of the Turbolet is to receive indigenous M-601-B turboprop of 740 eshp with which it was scheduled to commence flight testing during 1971. Latest modifications (see drawing) include redesigned wheel sponsons, a wider undercarriage track and revised engine nacelles.

LET L 410 TURBOLET

Dimensions: Span, 56 ft $1\frac{1}{4}$ in (17,10 m); length, 44 ft $7\frac{1}{2}$ in (13,61 m); height, 18 ft $0\frac{1}{2}$ in (5,50 m); wing area, 349·827 sq ft (32,5 m²).

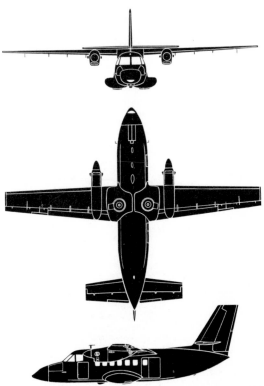

137

LOCKHEED 382G (L-100-30)

Country of Origin: USA.

Type: Medium- to long-range commercial cargo aircraft.

Power Plant: Four 4,508 eshp Allison 501-D22A turbo-props.

Performance: Max. cruise, 374 mph (602 km/h) at 25,000 ft (7 620 m); econ. cruise, 363 mph (584 km/h) at 28,000 ft (8 535 m); long-range cruise, 345 mph (555 km/h) at 28,000 ft (8 535 m); range with max. payload and 45 min reserves, 2,370 mls (3 814 km), with max. fuel, zero payload and same reserves, 4,830 mls (7 773 km).

Weights: Operational empty, 72,538 lb (32 903 kg); max. take-off, 155,000 lb (70 308 kg).

Accommodation: Normal flight crew of three and 6,057 cu ft (171,5 cu m) of cargo volume for loads of up to 45,000 lb (20 412 kg).

Status: First L-100-30 flown September 1970 with first deliveries (for Saturn Airways) in December 1970.

Notes: The L-100 is the commercial version of the military C-130 Hercules, variants including the Model 382B equivalent to the C-130E (see 1965 edition), the Model 328E (L-100-20) with a 100-in (2,54-m) fuselage stretch and 501-D22A engines, the Model 328F (L-100-20) with the lower-rated 501-D22s, and the Model 382G (L-100-30) with a further 80-in (2,03-m) stretch. Rear cargo windows, paratroop doors, and provision for JATO have been eliminated. Two L-100-20s are operated by the Kuwait Air Force.

LOCKHEED 382G (L-100-30)

Dimensions: Span, 132 ft 7 in (40,41 m); length, 112 ft 8½ in (34,35 m); height, 38 ft 3 in (11,66 m); wing area, 1,745 sq ft (162,12 m²).

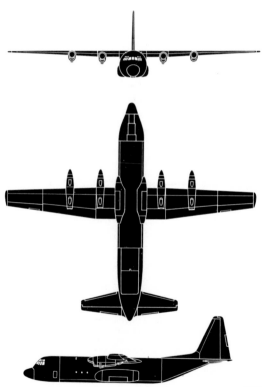

139

LOCKHEED C-5A GALAXY

Country of Origin: USA.
Type: Long-range military strategic transport.
Power Plant: Four 41,000 lb (18 600 kg) General Electric TF39-GE-1 turbofans.
Performance: Max. speed, 571 mph (919 km/h) at 25,000 ft (7 620 m); max. cruise at 525,000 lb (238 150 kg), 541 mph (871 km/h) at 30,000 ft (9 150 m); econ. cruise at 675,000 lb (306 175 kg), 537 mph (864 km/h) at 30,000 ft (9 150 m); range with max. fuel, 80,000-lb (36 287-kg) payload and reserves of 5% and 30 min, 6,500 mls (10 460 km), with max. payload and same reserves, 2,950 mls (4 745 km); initial climb at max. take-off, 2,300 ft/min (11,7 m/sec); service ceiling at 615,000 lb (278 950 kg), 34,000 ft (10 360 m).
Weights: Basic operational, 325,244 lb (147 528 kg); max. take-off, 764,500 lb (346 770 kg).
Accommodation: Basic flight crew of five plus relief crew and courier seating for 10. Seating for 75 troops on rear of upper deck, and provision for carrying 270 troops on lower deck. Typical freight loads include two M-60 tanks, an M-60 tank and two Iroquois helicopters, five M-113 personnel carriers, two Minutemen missiles on transporters, or 10 Pershing missiles with tow and launch vehicles.
Status: First of eight test and evaluation aircraft flown June 30, 1968, and first delivery to USAF made on December 17, 1969. Current orders for 81 C-5As scheduled for completion 1972.
Notes: USAF scheduled to have four C-5A squadrons.

LOCKHEED C-5A GALAXY

Dimensions: Span, 222 ft 8½ in (67,88 m); length, 247 ft 10 in (75,54 m); height, 65 ft 1½ in (19,85 m); wing area, 6,200 sq ft (576 m²).

LOCKHEED P-3C ORION

Country of Origin: USA.

Type: Long-range maritime patrol aircraft.

Power Plant: Four 4,910 eshp Allison T56-A-14W turbo-props.

Performance: Max. speed at 105,000 lb (47 625 kg), 476 mph (765 km/h) at 15,000 ft (4 570 m); normal cruise, 397 mph (639 km/h) at 25,000 ft (7 620 m); patrol speed, 230 mph (370 km/h) at 1,500 ft (457 m); loiter endurance (all engines) at 1,500 ft (457 m), 12·9 hrs, (two engines), 17 hrs; max. mission radius, 2,530 mls (4 075 km), with 3 hrs on station at 1,500 ft (457 m), 1,933 mls (3 110 km); service ceiling, 28,300 ft (8 625 m).

Weights: Empty, 62,000 lb (28 123 kg); normal max. take-off, 133,500 lb (60 558 kg); max. overload, 142,000 lb (64 410 kg).

Accommodation: Normal flight crew of 10 of which five housed in tactical compartment. Up to 50 combat troops and up to 4,000 lb (1 814 kg) of equipment may be carried in the emergency trooping role.

Armament: Weapons bay can house two Mk 101 nuclear depth bombs and four Mk 43, 44 or 46 torpedoes, or eight Mk 54 bombs. An external ordnance load of up to 13,713 lb (6 220 kg) may be carried by nine pylons.

Status: YP-3C prototype flown October 8, 1968, with P-3C production deliveries commencing to US Navy mid-1969.

Notes: The P-3C differs from the P-3A and -3B primarily in having more advanced sensor equipment. Twelve P-3As have been modified as EP-3Es for the electronic reconnaissance role, others have been adapted for the weather reconnaissance role as WP-3As, and a specially-equipped version, the RP-3D, is being used to map the earth's magnetic field.

LOCKHEED P-3C ORION

Dimensions: Span, 99 ft 8 in (30,37 m); length, 116 ft 10 in (35,61 m); height, 33 ft 8½ in (10,29 m); wing area, 1,300 sq ft (120,77 m²).

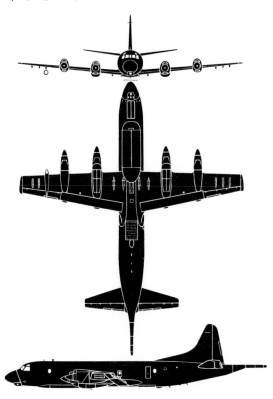

LOCKHEED F-104S STARFIGHTER

Country of Origin: USA.

Type: Single-seat interceptor and strike fighter.

Power Plant: One 11,870 lb (5 385 kg) dry and 17,900 lb (8 120 kg) reheat General Electric J79-GE-19 turbojet.

Performance: Max. speed, 910 mph (1 470 km/h) or Mach 1·2 at sea level, 1,450 mph (2 335 km/h) or Mach 2·2 at 36,000 ft (10 970 m); max. cruise, 610 mph (980 km/h) at 36,000 ft (10 970 m); tactical radius with two 162 Imp gal (736 l) and two 100 Imp gal (455 l) drop tanks, 740–775 mls (1 190–1 245 km); ferry range, 1,815 mls (2 920 km); initial climb, 50,000 plus ft/min (254 plus m/sec).

Weights: Empty, 14,573 lb (6 610 kg); loaded (clean), 21,307 lb (9 665 kg); max. take-off, 31,000 lb (14 060 kg).

Armament: One 20-mm M-61 rotary cannon, two AIM-7 Sparrow III and two AIM-9 Sidewinder AAMs.

Status: First of two Lockheed-built F-104S prototypes flown December 1966, and first Fiat-built production F-104S flown December 30, 1968. Production of 165 for Italian Air Force to be completed by end of 1972.

Notes: Derivative of the F-104G (see 1966 edition) optimised for all-weather intercept role. Features uprated engine with redesigned afterburner. Nine external stores attachment points. Primary armament is the Sparrow semi-active radar-homing AAM.

LOCKHEED F-104S STARFIGHTER

Dimensions: Span, 21 ft 11 in (6,68 m); length, 54 ft 9 in (16,69 m); height, 13 ft 6 in (4,11 m); wing area, 196·1 sq ft (18,22 m²).

LOCKHEED L-1011-1 TRISTAR

Country of Origin: USA.

Type: Short- to medium-range commercial transport.

Power Plant: Three 40,600 lb (18 415 kg) Rolls-Royce RB.211-22 turbofans.

Performance: (Estimated) Max. cruise at max. take-off weight, 590 mph (950 km/h) at 35,000 ft (10 670 m); econ. cruise, 540 mph (870 km/h) at 35,000 ft (10 670 m); range with max. fuel and 40,000 lb (18 145 kg) payload, 4,467 mls (7 189 km); range with max. payload comprising 256 passengers and 5,000 lb (2 270 kg) cargo, 2,878 mls (4 629 km); initial climb, 2,800 ft/min (14,2 m/sec); service ceiling, 35,000 ft (10 670 m).

Weights: Empty, 218,999 lb (99 336 kg); operational empty, 234,275 lb (106 265 kg); max. take-off, 426,000 lb (193 230 kg).

Accommodation: Basic flight crew of three–four. Typical passenger configuration provides 256 seats in a ratio of 20% first class and 80% coach class. An all-economy configuration provides for 345 passengers, while up to 400 will be accommodated in a high-density configuration.

Status: First L-1011-1 flown November 16, 1970. Second joined flight test programme February 15, 1971. First deliveries (to Eastern) scheduled for March 1972 by which time production rate is expected to be one aircraft per week.

Notes: The Model 193 (L-1011) TriStar is the first aircraft to employ the RB.211 engine, and a decision concerning an extended-range TriStar is expected during 1972.

LOCKHEED L-1011-1 TRISTAR

Dimensions: Span, 155 ft 4 in (47,34 m); length, 177 ft 8½ in (54,16 m); height, 55 ft 4 in (16,87 m); wing area, 3,755 sq ft (348,85 m²).

LOCKHEED S-3A VIKING

Country of Origin: USA.

Type: Four-seat shipboard anti-submarine aircraft.

Power Plant: Two 9,000 lb (4 082 kg) General Electric TF34-GE-2 turbofans.

Performance: (Estimated) Max. speed, 495 mph (797 km/h); max. cruise, 403 mph (649 km/h); typical loiter speed, 184 mph (257 km/h); max. ferry range, 3,500 mls (5 630 km) plus; service ceiling, 35,000 ft (10 670 m).

Weights: (Estimated) Empty equipped, 26,600 lb (12 065 kg); normal take-off, 42,000 lb (19 050 kg); max. take-off, 47,000 lb (21 320 kg).

Accommodation: Pilot and co-pilot side by side on flight deck, with tactical co-ordinator and sensor operator in aft cabin. All four crew members provided with zero-zero ejection seats.

Armament: Various combinations of torpedoes, depth charges, bombs and ASMs in internal weapons bay and on underwing pylons.

Status: First of eight development and evaluation aircraft was scheduled to commence its test programme in January 1972, and current US Navy planning calls for acquisition of 191 production aircraft during Fiscal Years 1972–75.

Notes: Intended as a successor to the Grumman S-2 Tracker in US Navy service, Lockheed's shipboard turbofan-powered ASW aircraft was selected for development mid-1969 after competitive evaluation of a number of proposals, and, subsequently designated S-3A, it is scheduled to enter fleet service early in 1974.

LOCKHEED S-3A VIKING

Dimensions: Span, 68 ft 8 in (20,93 m); length, 53 ft 4 in (16,26 m); height, 22 ft 9 in (6,93 m); wing area, 598 sq ft (55,56 m²).

LOCKSPEISER LDA-01

Country of Origin: United Kingdom.
Type: General purpose and utility aircraft.
Power Plant: One 85 hp Continental C85-12 four-cylinder horizontally-opposed engine.
Performance: (Estimated for proposed full-scale version) Normal cruise, 152 mph (245 km/h); range, 403 mls (649 km); ferry range (with auxiliary fuel), 1,730 mls (2 785 km); normal endurance, 2·8 hrs; initial climb, 1,280 ft/min (6,5 m/sec).
Weights: Empty equipped, 1,300 lb (590 kg); (full-scale version) empty equipped, 1,500 lb (680 kg); max. take-off, 4,500 lb (2 041 kg).
Accommodation: (Full-scale version) Pilot and six passengers or two casualty stretchers and two medical attendants.
Status: The 7/10ths scale prototype flew for the first time on August 24, 1971.
Notes: The LDA-01 is a 7/10ths scale flying model of the Lockspeiser Land Development Aircraft which is intended to be powered by a 340 hp Lycoming O-540 six-cylinder engine. The full-size aircraft will have a payload of 1 ton, and emphasis has been placed on simplicity and ease of maintenance. The tandem-wing arrangement has been selected for the wide CG range and greater tolerance in load distribution that it offers. Central fin discarded after initial trials.

LOCKSPEISER LDA-01

Dimensions: Span, 29 ft 0 in (8,84 m); length, 22 ft 6 in (6,85 m); (full-scale version) span, 44 ft 0 in (13,41 m); length, 34 ft 6 in (10,51 m); height, 12 ft 3 in (3,72 m).

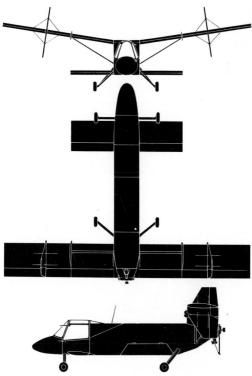

McDONNELL DOUGLAS DC-8 SUPER 63

Country of Origin: USA.

Type: Long-range commercial transport.

Power Plant: Four 19,000 lb (8 618 kg) Pratt & Whitney JT3D-7 turbofans.

Performance: Max. cruise at 220,000 lb (99 800 kg), 583 mph (938 km/h) at 30,000 ft (9 150 m); long-range cruise, 512 mph (825 km/h) at 35,000 ft (10 700 m); range with max. payload and normal reserves, 4,500 mls (7 240 km), with max. fuel, 6,930 mls (11 150 km); initial climb, 2,165 ft/min (11 m/sec).

Weights: Basic operational, 153,749 lb (69 739 kg); max. take-off, 350,000 lb (158 760 kg).

Accommodation: Normal flight crew of four and up to 251 economy-class passengers plus 14,000 lb (6 350 kg) of freight.

Status: First DC-8 Super 63 flown April 10, 1967. Only Super 62 and 63 variants of the DC-8 remained in production at beginning of 1972 when approximately 553 DC-8s of all versions had been delivered.

Notes: The Super 63 is the ultimate development of the DC-8 family, being a combination of the fuselage stretch introduced by the Super 61, the aerodynamic improvements of the shorter-fuselage Super 62, and more powerful turbojets. All-cargo and cargo-passenger versions are known as the Super 63AF and 63CF (illustrated above) Jet Trader, max. take-off weight being raised to 355,000 lb. (161 028 kg). Similar variants exist of the Super 62 which has 18,000 lb (8 172 kg) JT3D-3B turbofans and a length of 157 ft 5 in (47,98 m).

152

McDONNELL DOUGLAS DC-8 SUPER 63

Dimensions: Span, 148 ft 5 in (45,23 m); length, 187 ft 4¾ in (57,12 m); height, 42 ft 5 in (12,92 m); wing area, 2,926·8 sq ft (271,9 m²).

McDONNELL DOUGLAS DC-9 SERIES 40

Country of Origin: USA.

Type: Short- to medium-range commercial transport.

Power Plant: Two 15,000 lb (6 804 kg) Pratt & Whitney JT8D-9 turbofans.

Performance: Max. cruise, 561 mph (903 km/h) at 27,000 ft (8 230 m); econ. cruise, 535 mph (860 km/h) at 33,000 ft (10 060 m); range cruise, 500 mph (805 km/h) at 35,000 ft (10 670 m); range at max. cruise with reserves for 230 mls (370 km) and 60 min hold, 1,192 mls (1 918 km), at range cruise with same reserves, 1,685 mls (2 710 km).

Weights: Empty, 59,690 lb (25 261 kg); max. take-off, 114,000 lb (51 710 kg).

Accommodation: Normal flight crew of two–three, and maximum of 125 tourist-class passengers in five-abreast seating.

Status: Series 40 first flown November 28, 1967, with first delivery (to SAS) following February 29, 1968. Deliveries of all models of the DC-9 totalled some 650 by the beginning of 1972 with 680 on order.

Notes: The DC-9-40 is a stretched version of the -30 (see 1968 edition) with more powerful turbofans and increased fuel capacity. A USAF aeromedical evacuation transport derivative of the DC-9-30 is known as the C-9A Nightingale (see 1969 edition), 21 examples having been ordered. Other models are the DC-9-10 (see 1966 edition), this being the initial basic version, and the DC-9-20 (see 1970 edition) for operation in hot-and-high conditions, combining the short (104 ft $4\frac{3}{4}$ in/31,82 m) fuselage of the -10 with the longer-span wing of the -30 and -40.

McDONNELL DOUGLAS DC-9 SERIES 40

Dimensions: Span, 93 ft 5 in (28,47 m); length, 125 ft 7¼ in (38,28 m); height, 28 ft 0 in (8,53 m); wing area, 1,000·7 sq ft (92,97 m²).

McDONNELL DOUGLAS DC-10 SERIES 10

Country of Origin: USA.

Type: Short- to medium-range commercial transport.

Power Plant: Three 40,000 lb (18 144 kg) General Electric CF6-6 turbofans.

Performance: Max, cruise, 578 mph (930 km/h) at 31,000 ft (9 450 m); range cruise, 520 mph (837 km/h) at 31,000 ft (9 450 m); range with max. payload, 2,429 mls (3 909 km) at 540 mph (870 km/h) at 35,000 ft (10 670 m), with max. fuel, 5,147 mls (8 283 km).

Weights: Operational empty, 231,779 lb (105 142 kg); max. take-off, 430,000 lb (195 045 kg).

Accommodation: Basic flight crew of three-four. Typical mixed-class arrangement will provide for 48 first-class and 222 coach-class passengers in six-abreast and eight-abreast seating respectively. A 332-passenger all-tourist arrangement is available.

Status: First DC-10 flown on August 29, 1970, and first deliveries (to American and United) effected on July 29, 1971. Twelve DC-10s were to have been delivered by the end of 1971 with a production tempo of two per month being attained late 1972.

Notes: Developments of the initial Series 10 include the extended-range Series 20 and a more powerful equivalent, the Series 30 with 48,100 lb (21 817 kg) CF6-50A engines. First deliveries of the Series 30 (to the KSSU consortium) scheduled for 1972.

156

McDONNELL DOUGLAS DC-10 SERIES 10

Dimensions: Span, 155 ft 4 in (47,35 m); length, 181 ft 5 in (55,29 m); height, 58 ft 1 in (17,70 m); wing area, 3,550 sq ft (329,8 m²).

McDONNELL DOUGLAS (F-4M) PHANTOM F.G.R. MK. 2

Country of Origin: USA.

Type: Two-seat all-weather multi-purpose fighter.

Power Plant: Two 12,250 lb (5 556 kg) dry and 20,515 lb (9 305 kg) reheat Rolls-Royce RB.168-25R Spey Mk. 202 turbofans.

Performance: Max. speed, 910 mph (1 464 km/h) or Mach 1·2 at 1,000 ft (305 m), 1,386 mph (2 230 km/h) or Mach 2·1 at 40,000 ft (12 190 m); tactical radius with six 1,000-lb (453,6-kg) bombs and two 308 Imp gal (1 400 l) drop tanks for hi-lo-hi mission profile, 550 mls (885 km), lo-lo-hi mission profile, 380 mls (610 km); ferry range with max. external fuel, 2,500 mls (4 023 km).

Weights: Approx. empty equipped, 30,000 lb (13 610 kg); approx. normal loaded, 49,000 lb (22 225 kg); max. take-off, 58,000 lb (26 310 kg).

Armament: (Intercept) One 20-mm M-61A1 rotary cannon in SUU 23A centreline pod, four AIM-7E Sparrow IIIB and four AIM-9D Sidewinder IC AAMs, or (attack) 11 1,000-lb (453,6-kg) Mk. 14 bombs, 10 Matra pods each with 18 68-mm rockets, Martel ASMs, etc.

Status: First of two (YF-4M) prototypes flown February 17, 1967, and deliveries of 146 (F-4M) to RAF commenced July 1968 and completed October 1969.

Notes: Anglicised shore-based equivalent of US Navy's F-4J for RAF. Shipboard interceptor equivalent for the Royal Navy, the (F-4K) Phantom F.G. Mk. 1 (24 delivered). EMI reconnaissance pod provided for RAF Phantoms during 1971.

McDONNELL DOUGLAS (F-4M) PHANTOM
F.G.R. MK. 2

Dimensions: Span, 38 ft 4¾ in (11,70 m); length, 57 ft 11 in (17,65 m); height, 16 ft 3⅓ in (4,96 m); wing area, 530 sq ft (49,2 m²).

McDONNELL DOUGLAS RF-4E
PHANTOM II

Country of Origin: USA.

Type: Two-seat tactical reconnaissance aircraft.

Power Plant: Two 11,870 lb (5 385 kg) dry and 17,900 lb (8 120 kg) reheat General Electric J79-GE-17 turbojets.

Performance: Max. speed without external stores, 910 mph (1 464 km/h) or Mach 1·2 at 1,000 ft (305 m), 1,500 mph (2 414 km/h) or Mach 2·27 at 40,000 ft (12 190 m); tactical radius for hi-lo-hi mission profile with one 500 Imp gal (2 273 l) and two 308 Imp gal (1 400 l) drop tanks, 685 mls (1 100 km); max. ferry range, 2,300 mls (3 700 km) at 575 mph (925 km/h) at 40,000 ft (12 190 m).

Weights: Normal loaded, 46,076 lb (20 900 kg); max. take-off, 57,320 lb (26 000 kg).

Status: First production RF-4Es (six to Israel) delivered 1969, and first deliveries (of 88) to Federal Germany initiated November 1970.

Notes: The RF-4E is a multi-sensor reconnaissance version of the F-4E multi-purpose fighter (see 1970 edition) with the same engines, equipment standards being similar to those of the USAF's RF-4C (see 1965 edition) apart (in the case of Federal Germany's RF-4Es) from having a more advanced Goodyear side-looking radar and a data transfer system beaming reconnaissance data to ground stations. The *Luft-waffe's* RF-4Es will equip four 15-aircraft *Staffeln* which will operate from Bremgarten and Leck from late 1971. It is anticipated that 20 RF-4Es will be purchased during the early 'seventies to replace RF-86F Sabres serving with the Japanese Air Self-Defence Force. The US Marine Corps reconnaissance version of the Phantom is designated RF-4B.

McDONNELL DOUGLAS RF-4E PHANTOM II

Dimensions: Span, 38 ft $4\frac{3}{4}$ in (11,70 m); length, 62 ft $10\frac{1}{2}$ in (19,20 m); height, 16 ft $3\frac{1}{3}$ in (4,96 m); wing area, 530 sq ft (49,2 m^2).

McDONNELL DOUGLAS F-15

Country of Origin: USA.

Type: Single-seat air superiority fighter.

Power Plant: Two (approx.) 24,000 lb (10 886 kg) reheat Pratt & Whitney F100-PW-101 turbofans.

Performance: Max. speed (approx.) 1,650 mph (2 655 km/h) or Mach 2·5 above 40,000 ft (12 190 m), 915 mph (1 470 km/h) or Mach 1·2 at 1,000 ft (305 m).

Weights: (Estimated) Normal loaded, 40,000 lb (18 144 kg); max. take-off, 56,000 lb (25 400 kg).

Armament: One 20-mm M-61A-1 rotary cannon (eventually to be replaced by 25-mm GAU-7/A rotary cannon) and mix of AIM-7F Sparrow and AIM-9X Sidewinder AAMs.

Status: First of 20 development and test F-15s scheduled to enter flight test phase in July 1972. Eight to be used for service evaluation and 12 for contractor's test programme. Initial production order expected to call for 87 aircraft with deliveries to USAF commencing during 1975, eventual total buy possibly exceeding 700 aircraft.

Notes: McDonnell Douglas was named prime airframe contractor for the F-15 air superiority fighter on 23 December 1969, the primary purpose of this warplane being that of matching the manœuvrability, acceleration and weapons capability of the latest generation of Soviet high-performance fighters currently under development. A two-seat training version of the F-15 is envisaged but this may be eliminated from the programme. The F-15 is expected to provide the USAF with its principal air superiority capability during the period 1975–85.

McDONNELL DOUGLAS F-15

Dimensions: Span, 42 ft 10 in (13,06 m); length, 63 ft 10 in (19,46 m); height, 18 ft 7 in (5,67 m).

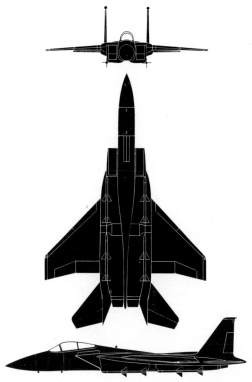

McDONNELL DOUGLAS A-4M SKYHAWK

Country of Origin: USA.

Type: Single-seat light attack bomber.

Power Plant: One 11,200 lb (5 080 kg) Pratt & Whitney J52-P-408A turbojet.

Performance: Max. speed without external stores, 685 mph (1 102 km/h) or Mach 0·9 at sea level, 640 mph (1 030 km/h) at 25,000 ft (7 620 m), in high drag configuration, 625 mph (1 080 km/h) or Mach 0·82 at sea level, 605 mph (973 km/h) or Mach 0·84 at 30,000 ft (9 145 m); combat radius on internal fuel for hi-lo-lo-hi mission profile with 4,000 lb (1 814 kg) of external stores, 340 mls (547 km); initial climb, 15,850 ft/min (80,5 m/sec), at 23,000 lb (10 433 kg), 8,440 ft/min (42,7 m/sec).

Weights: Empty, 10,600 lb (4 808 kg); max. take-off, 24,500 lb (11 113 kg).

Armament: Two 20-mm Mk. 12 cannon with 200 rpg. Maximum of 9,195 lb (4 170 kg) stores externally.

Status: First of two A-4M prototypes flown April 10, 1970, and first aircraft for USMC delivered November 3, 1970.

Notes: A-4M is basically similar to the A-4F (see 1970 edition), apart from new avionics and more powerful turbojet, offering improved short-field capability, combat manoeuvrability, climb and acceleration. Cannon ammunition capacity has been doubled and cockpit canopy enlarged.

164

McDONNELL DOUGLAS A-4M SKYHAWK

Dimensions: Span, 27 ft 6 in (8,38 m); length, 40 ft 3$\frac{1}{4}$ in (12,27 m); height, 15 ft 0 in (4,57 m); wing area, 260 sq ft (24,16 m^2).

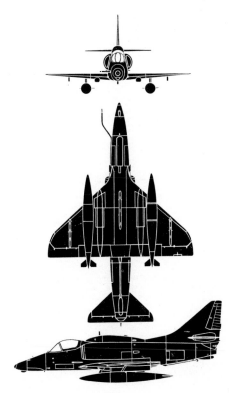

MIKOYAN MIG-21MF (FISHBED-J)

Country of Origin: USSR.

Type: Single-seat multi-purpose fighter.

Power Plant: One 11,244 lb (5 100 kg) dry and 14,550 lb (6 600 kg) Tumansky R-11 turbojet.

Performance: Max. speed, 808 mph (1 300 km/h) or Mach 1·06 at 1,000 ft (305 m), 1,386 mph (2 230 km/h) or Mach 2·1 above 36,090 ft (11 000 m); range on internal fuel, 683 mls (1 100 km); ferry range with max. external fuel, 1,118 mls (1 800 km); service ceiling, 59,055 ft (18 000 m).

Weights: Normal take-off (with four K-13 AAMs), 18,078 lb (8 200 kg), (with two K-13s and two 110 Imp gal/500 l drop tanks), 19,731 lb (8950 kg); max. take-off (with two K-13s and three drop tanks), 20,723 lb (9 400 kg).

Armament: Two 23-mm cannon with 100 rpg in fuselage and up to four K-13 (Atoll) AAMs on wing pylons for intercept role. Four 550-lb (250-kg) bombs or four 220-mm or 325-mm ASMs.

Status: The MiG-21MF is a progressive development of the MiG-21PFM (*Fishbed-D*), and entered service with the Soviet Air Forces in the late 'sixties. Manufactured in parallel is a reconnaissance version (*Fishbed-H*), and licence manufacture of the MiG-21PF (early *Fishbed-D*) is undertaken by HAL in India.

Notes: The MiG-21MF is equipped with a boundary layer blowing system known as SPS. The *Fishbed-C* (MiG-21F) and -*E* are clear-weather interceptors, and the reconnaissance *Fishbed-H* features wingtip ECM fairings.

MIKOYAN MIG-21MF (FISHBED-J)

Dimensions: Span, 23 ft $5\frac{1}{2}$ in (7,15 m); length (including probe), 51 ft $8\frac{1}{2}$ in (15,76 m), (without probe), 44 ft 2 in (13,46 m); wing area, 247·57 sq ft (23 m²).

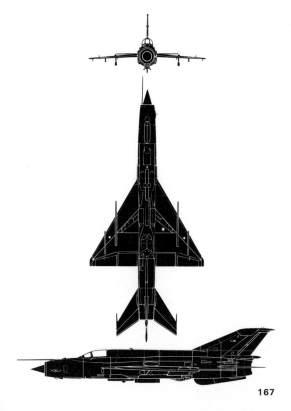

MIKOYAN MIG-23 (FOXBAT)

Country of Origin: USSR.
Type: Single-seat interceptor, strike and reconnaissance fighter.
Power Plant: Two (approx.) 24,250 lb (11 000 kg) reheat Tumansky turbojets.
Performance: (Estimated) Max. short-period dash speed, 2,100 mph (3 380 km/h) or Mach 3·2 at 39,370 ft (12 000 m); max. sustained speed, 1,780 mph (2 865 km/h) or Mach 2·7 at 39,370 ft (12 000 m), 975 mph (1 570 km/h) or Mach 1·3 at 4,920 ft (1 500 m); normal combat radius, 700 mls (1 125 km); time to 36,000 ft (10 970 m), 2·5 min.
Weights: (Estimated) Empty equipped, 34,000 lb (15 420 kg); normal loaded, 50,000–55,000 lb (22 680–24 950 kg); max. take-off, 64,200 lb (29 120 kg).
Armament: Four wing stations for *Atoll* semi-active homing AAMs.
Status: Believed flown in prototype form 1963–64 with service deliveries following from 1967–68.
Notes: The MiG-23 multi-purpose fighter has established a number of FAI-recognised records since 1965 under the designation Ye-266. On October 5, 1967, the Ye-266 established a record of 1,852·61 mph (2 981,5 km/h), or Mach 2·8, over a 310-mile (500-km) closed circuit, following this on October 27 with a speed of 1,841·81 mph (2 920,67 km/h), or Mach 2·7, over a 621-mile (1 000-km) circuit.

MIKOYAN MIG-23 (FOXBAT)

Dimensions: (Estimated) Span, 41 ft 0 in (12,5 m); length, 70 ft 0 in (21,33 m).

MITSUBISHI MU-2J

Country of Origin: Japan.

Type: Light business executive and utility transport.

Power Plant: Two 715 shp Garrett AiResearch TPE 331-6-251M turboprops.

Performance: Max. cruise, 345 mph (555 km/h) at 10,000 ft (3 050 m); econ. cruise, 304 mph (490 km/h) at 20,000 ft (6 100 m); max. range with 30 min reserves, 1,553 mls (2 500 km) at 22,965 ft (7 000 m); initial climb, 2,697 ft/min (13,7 m/sec); service ceiling, 30,775 ft (9 380 m).

Weights: Empty equipped, 6,800 lb (3 085 kg); max. take-off, 10,802 lb (4 900 kg).

Accommodation: Normal flight crew of two, and various cabin arrangements providing accommodation for from four to 12 passengers.

Status: Prototype MU-2J flown August 1970, deliveries of this model commencing late 1971. Parallel civil production models are the MU-2F and MU-2G, and final assembly of most civil aircraft is undertaken at San Angelo, Texas.

Notes: MU-2J is a more powerful version of the MU-2G (see 1971 edition) which, in turn, was a stretched variant of the MU-2F (see 1969 edition) with a re-positioned nosewheel and external main undercarriage fairings. The engines of the MU-2J are flat-rated at 665 hp up to 12,000 ft (3 660 m), and these are also employed by the latest short-fuselage model, the MU-2K, which is otherwise similar to the MU-2F. Some 220 MU-2s of all versions had been delivered by the beginning of 1972.

MITSUBISHI MU-2J

Dimensions: Span, 39 ft 2 in (11,95 m); length, 59 ft 5¾ in (12,03 m); height, 13 ft 8¼ in (4,17 m); wing area, 178 sq ft (16,55 m²).

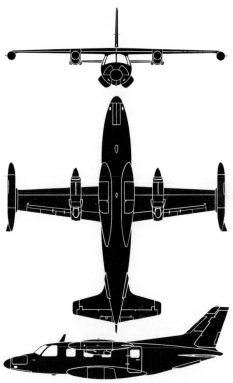

MITSUBISHI XT-2

Country of Origin: Japan.
Type: Tandem two-seat advanced trainer.
Power Plant: Two 4,600 lb (2 086 kg) dry and 6,950 lb (3 150 kg) reheat Rolls-Royce Turboméca RB.172-T.260 Adour turbofans.
Performance: (Estimated) Max. speed, 1,056 mph (1 700 km/h) or Mach 1·6 at 40,000 ft (12 190 m); max. ferry range, 1,600 mls (2 575 km); service ceiling, 50,000 ft.
Weights: (Estimated) Normal take-off, 21,000 lb (9 525 kg).
Armament: Provision for one 20-mm rotary cannon internally and various external ordnance loads on fuselage, underwing, and wingtip stations.
Status: First of two flying prototypes was flown on July 20, 1971. Current plans call for deliveries of 50 production T-2A trainers to commence 1973, with a follow-on order for a further 30 aircraft.
Notes: Japan's first indigenous supersonic aircraft, the T-2A trainer is intended to enter the inventory of the Air Self-Defence Force in 1974. The basic design is also intended to fulfil operational roles, and the ASDF has a requirement for 50 examples of a close-support fighter version, currently referred to as the SF-X, and for 20 examples of a short-range tactical reconnaissance model, the RF-X2, these entering the inventory from 1975 onwards. The first ASDF training squadron to receive the T-2A is scheduled to be formed during 1974, F-86F Sabres and T-33As currently used for advanced training being progressively withdrawn.

MITSUBISHI XT-2

Dimensions: Span, 25 ft 11 in (7,90 m); length, 58 ft 4¾ in (17,80 m); height, 14 ft 9¼ in (4,50 m); wing area, 228·2 sq ft (21,2 m²).

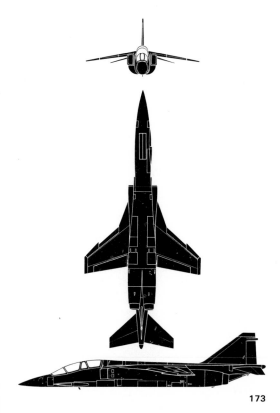

NORTH AMERICAN ROCKWELL
AERO COMMANDER 111

Country of Origin: USA.
Type: Light cabin monoplane.
Power Plant: One 180 hp Lycoming O-360-A1G6 four-cylinder horizontally-opposed engine.
Performance: Max. speed, 150 mph (241 km/h); max. cruise, 142 mph (228 km/h) at 7,500 ft (2 286 m); initial climb, 750 ft/min (3,8 m/sec); service ceiling, 14,500 ft (4 420 m); optimum range, 1,010 mls (1 625 km).
Weights: Empty, 1,138 lb (516 kg); max. loaded, 2,500 lb (1 134 kg).
Accommodation: Pilot and three passengers seated in pairs.
Status: First Model 111 flown September 1971 with FAA certification scheduled for early 1972. Production rate of three Models 111 and 112 per day planned by end of 1972.
Notes: The Model 111 is a version of the Model 112 first flown on December 4, 1970, and differing in having a fully retractable tricycle undercarriage. Deliveries of the Model 112 were scheduled to commence early 1972 with deliveries of the Model 111 commencing six months later. By 1973 a twin-engined version of the basic design is to be made available, and this is to be followed by six-seat versions of all three models with more powerful engines.

NORTH AMERICAN ROCKWELL
AERO COMMANDER 111

Dimensions: Span, 32 ft 9 in (9,98 m); length, 24 ft 10 in (7,57 m); height, 8 ft 5 in (2,51 m); wing area, 152 sq ft (14,12 m²).

NORTH AMERICAN ROCKWELL
OV-10 BRONCO

Country of Origin: USA.

Type: Tandem two-seat (OV-10A) multi-purpose counter-insurgency and (OV-10B) target-towing aircraft.

Power Plant: Two 715 shp Garrett AiResearch T76-G-10/12 turboprops and (OV-10B) one 2,950 lb (1 339 kg) General Electric J85-GE-4 auxiliary turbojet.

Performance: (OV-10A) Max. speed without external stores, 279 mph (449 km/h) at sea level, 259 mph (417 km/h) at 20,000 ft (6 095 m); average cruise, 194 mph (312 km/h); tactical radius for close support mission at 12,500 lb (5 670 kg), 228 mls (367 km); ferry range, 1,380 mls (2 220 km).

Weights: (OV-10A) Empty, 7,190 lb (3 260 kg); normal take-off, 12,500 lb (5 670 kg); max. overload take-off, 14,444 lb (6 552 kg).

Armament: Four 7,62-mm M-60C machine guns with 500 rpg. Max. weapon load of 3,600 lb (1 633 kg) distributed between four 600-lb (272-kg) capacity and one 1,200-lb (544-kg) capacity external stations (on sponsons and beneath fuselage). Two 500-lb (227-kg) wing stations optional.

Status: First of seven prototypes flown July 16, 1965. Production for US services comprising 157 for USAF and 114 for USMC completed April 1969. Manufacture resumed mid-1969 against order for 18 (OV-10B) for Federal Germany followed by 16 (OV-10C) for Thailand, and again late 1971 against order for 16 (OV-10E) from Venezuela.

Notes: Twelve of 18 OV-10B target-tugs delivered to Germany are fitted with an auxiliary turbojet (illustrated).

176

NORTH AMERICAN ROCKWELL OV-10 BRONCO

Dimensions: Span, 40 ft 0 in (12,19 m); length, 39 ft 10 in (12,14 m); height, 15 ft 1 in (4,59 m); wing area, 291 sq ft (27,03 m²).

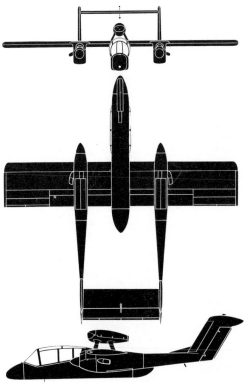

NORTH AMERICAN ROCKWELL SABRE 75

Country of Origin: USA.

Type: Light business executive transport.

Power Plant: Two 3,300 lb (1 497 kg) Pratt & Whitney JT12A-8 turbojets.

Performance: Max. cruise, 563 mph (906 km/h) at 21,550 ft (6 550 m); econ. cruise, 462 mph (743 km/h) at 39,000–45,000 ft (11 890–13 715 m); service ceiling, 45,000 ft (13 715 m); range with six passengers and normal reserves, 1,860 mls (2 995 km).

Weights: Operational empty, 11,980 lb (5 435 kg); max. take-off, 21,000 lb (9 525 kg).

Accommodation: Normal flight crew of two and various arrangements for six to 10 passengers.

Status: Evolved from the Sabreliner, the Sabre 75 was first introduced in June 1971 with production deliveries commencing in the same year.

Notes: The Sabre 75 is a development of the Sabreliner Series 60 (see 1968 edition), utilising the same wings, tail unit and power plant, and marrying these to a new fuselage of deeper section offering increased cabin headroom. Other features include dual-wheel undercarriage members and square cabin windows. Being manufactured in parallel, the Sabre Commander is essentially similar to the Sabreliner Series 60 but possesses many of the refinements of the Sabre 75. The Sabre Commander is basically a nine-seater and is being marketed completely equipped. The basic Sabreliner has been in continuous production for 14 years.

NORTH AMERICAN ROCKWELL SABRE 75

Dimensions: Span, 44 ft 5¼ in (13,54 m); length, 47 ft 0 in (14,32 m); height, 17 ft 3 in (5,26 m); wing area, 342 sq ft (31,78 m²).

NORTHROP YA-9A

Country of Origin: USA.

Type: Single-seat close-support and attack aircraft.

Power Plant: Two 6,000 lb (2 722 kg) Avco Lycoming ALF 502 turbofans.

Performance: (Estimated) Max. speed in excess of 460 mph (740 km/h); endurance with 16,000 lb (7 257 kg) of external ordnance, up to 4 hrs.

Weights: (Estimated) Operational empty, 17,200 lb (7 802 kg); max. take-off, 39,570 lb (17 948 kg).

Armament: One 30-mm cannon with 1,350 rounds and max. external ordnance load of 16,000 lb (7 257 kg). Typical external loads to comprise 24 500-lb (227-kg) Mk 82 bombs, 16 750-lb (340-kg) M 117 bombs, four 2,000-lb (907-kg) Mk 84 bombs, 20 Rockeye II cluster bombs, or nine AGM-65 Maverick ASMs.

Status: Two YA-9As ordered December 1970 for competititive evaluation with Fairchild YA-10A (see page 90), both YA-9As being scheduled to commence flight testing in June 1972. Anticipated USAAF orders for 600 of selected aircraft.

Notes: The YA-9A has been designed to meet the requirements of the USAF's A-X (Attack-Experimental) specification, primary objectives of the programme being low cost, and high effectiveness and survivability. The YA-9A is to operate from short battlefield-area airstrips, taking off within 1,000 ft (305 m) with a reasonable payload. A 12-month USAF evaluation of the YA-9A and YA-10A is expected to commence in November 1972.

NORTHROP YA-9A

Dimensions: Span, 57 ft 0 in (17,37 m); length, 53 ft 6 in (16,31 m); height, 17 ft 10 in (5,43 m); wing area, 550 sq ft (51,1 m²).

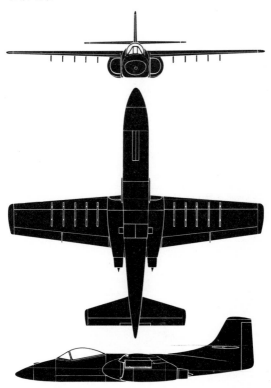

NORTHROP F-5E TIGER II

Country of Origin: USA.

Type: Single-seat air-superiority fighter.

Power Plant: Two 3,500 lb (1 588 kg) dry and 5,000 lb (2 268 kg) reheat General Electric J85-GE-21 turbojets.

Performance: Max. speed (clean), 1,055 mph (1 710 km/h) or Mach 1·6 at 40,000 ft (12 190 m), with two AIM-9 AAMs, 983 mph (1 582 km/h); combat radius with two AIM-9 AAMs, 178 mls (286 km), with 229 Imp gal (1 040 l) centreline drop tank and two AIM-9 AAMs, 434 mls (698 km); ferry range, 1,595 mls (2 567 km); initial climb at 13,220 lb (5 997 kg), 31,600 ft/min (160,52 m/sec); combat ceiling, 53,500 ft (16 310 m).

Weights: Loaded (air-to-air mission), 15,660 lb (7 103 kg); max. take-off, 21,818 lb (9 896 kg).

Armament: Two 20-mm M-39 cannon with 280 rpg and (air-to-air mission) two wingtip-mounted AIM-9 Sidewinder AAMs. Max. ordnance load, 7,000 lb (3 175 kg).

Status: Selected as winning contender in USAF's International Fighter Aircraft (IFA) contest in November 1970, and current plans call for procurement of 325 aircraft under the Military Assistance Programme for supply to Thailand, Taiwan, South Vietnam and South Korea. First of five test and development F-5Es scheduled to fly September 1972 with first production deliveries commencing May 1973. Thirty F-5Es (plus 20 two-seat F-5Bs) ordered by Saudi Arabia.

Notes: The F-5E is a more powerful derivative of the F-5A (see 1970 edition) with air intercept radar, increased internal fuel capacity, and various aerodynamic refinements. The F-5E is expected to enter service with foreign air forces during the course of 1974.

182

NORTHROP F-5E TIGER II

Dimensions: Span, 26 ft 6 in (8,08 m); length, 48 ft 2 in (14,68 m); height, 13 ft 2 in (4,01 m); wing area, 186·2 sq ft (17,29 m²).

PARTENAVIA P.68 VICTOR

Country of Origin: Italy.
Type: Light utility transport.
Power Plant: Two 200 hp Lycoming IO-360-A1B four-cylinder horizontally-opposed engines.
Performance: Max. speed, 201 mph (324 km/h) at sea level; cruise at 75% power, 196 mph (316 km/h) at 8,200 ft (2 500 m), at 65% power, 194 mph (313 km/h) at 11,810 ft (3 600 m); range at 65% power with 30 min reserves at 55% power, 932 mls (1 500 km); initial climb, 1,850 ft/min (9,4 m/sec); service ceiling, 26,575 ft (8 100 m).
Weights: Empty, 2,216 lb (1 005 kg); max. take-off, 3,878 lb (1 760 kg).
Accommodation: Seating for pilot and five passengers in three pairs of side-by-side seats. Dual controls provided as standard equipment.
Status: First prototype flown on May 25, 1970, 10 pre-production aircraft completed, and production to attain three per month during 1972. The P.68 is being offered with either 180 or 200 hp engines and either fixed or retractable undercarriage.
Notes: Placing emphasis on simplicity and ease of maintenance and operation, the P.68 possesses short-field capability and has been designed to fulfil such roles as air taxi, light utility transport, and ambulance. Modular design will permit manufacture of several variants without major changes in production facilities.

184

PARTENAVIA P.68 VICTOR

Dimensions: Span, 39 ft 4½ in (12,00 m); length, 29 ft 11 in (9,12 m); height, 10 ft 8 in (3,25 m); wing area, 200·2 sq ft (18,6 m²).

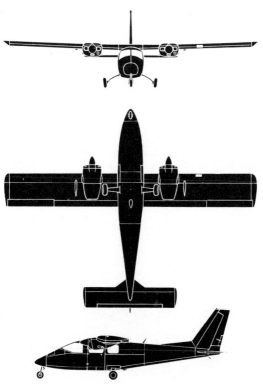

PIPER PE-1 ENFORCER

Country of Origin: USA.

Type: Single-seat counter-insurgency and strike aircraft.

Power Plant: One 2,535 hp Lycoming T55-L-9 turboprop.

Performance: Max. speed (clean condition), 460 mph (740 km/h) at 20,000 ft (6 096 m), with typical external ordnance load, 432 mph (695 km/h); max. cruise, 370 mph (595 km/h); max. range, 2,994 mls (4 820 km).

Weights: Approx. max. take-off, 14,000 lb (6 350 kg).

Armament: Six wing-mounted 0·5-in (12,7-mm) machine guns and 6–10 external hardpoints for various combinations of gun pods, bombs and ASMs.

Status: First of two prototypes flown on April 29, 1971, second prototype following in June 1971.

Notes: The PE-1 Enforcer is a structurally-redesigned, newly-tooled development of the WW II North American P-51 Mustang, and is essentially a new aircraft, having no component commonality with the original Mustang. Development of the Enforcer was taken over by the Piper Aircraft Corporation from Cavalier Aircraft in 1970, and this type participated in 1971 in the *Pave Coin* Programme of the USAF to select suitable aircraft for supply to smaller air forces under the Military Assistance Programme. Armour protection is provided for both pilot and engine, provision is made for an ejection seat, and additional wing spars permit up to 10 hardpoints for external ordnance loads. An earlier turboprop-driven derivative of the P-51 was the Cavalier Turbo Mustang III (see 1969 edition) with a Rolls-Royce Dart.

PIPER PE-1 ENFORCER

Dimensions: Span (over tiptanks), 40 ft 1½ in (12,23 m); length, 32 ft 10 in (10,00 m); height, 8 ft 10 in (2,69 m); wing area, 233 sq ft (21,65 m²).

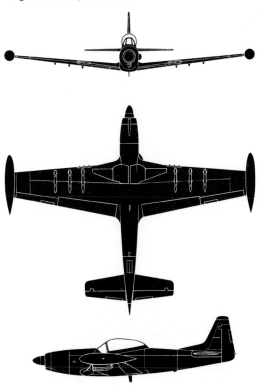

PIPER PA-31 TURBO NAVAJO B

Country of Origin: USA.

Type: Light business executive transport.

Power Plant: Two 310 hp Lycoming TIO-540-A six-cylinder horizontally-opposed engines.

Performance: Max. speed, 261 mph (420 km/h) at 15,000 ft (4 572 m); max. cruise, 251 mph (404 km/h) at 24,000 ft (7 315 m); econ. cruise, 209 mph (336 km/h) at 24,000 ft (7 315 m); range at max. cruise with 45 min reserves, 1,110 mls (1 786 km), at econ. cruise, 1,540 mls (2 478 km); initial climb, 1,445 ft/min (7,33 m/sec); service ceiling, 26,300 ft (8 016 m).

Weights: Empty equipped, 3,849 lb (1 746 kg); max. take-off, 6,500 lb (2 948 kg).

Accommodation: Standard arrangement for six individual seats in pairs with optional arrangements for up to nine persons.

Status: Turbo Navajo B introduced September 1971 as successor to the initial Turbo Navajo, the prototype of which was flown in March 1968 with production deliveries commencing in March 1970. Some 800 Navajos and Turbo Navajos delivered between 1967 and the beginning of 1972.

Notes: The Turbo Navajo B is a progressive refinement of the initial production Turbo Navajo (see 1971 edition), which, in turn, was a pressurised equivalent of the PA-31-300 Navajo (see 1968 edition). The original non-pressurised PA-31 was flown on September 30, 1964, deliveries of this type having commenced in April 1967.

PIPER PA-31 TURBO NAVAJO B

Dimensions: Span, 40 ft 8 in (12,40 m); length, 32 ft 7½ in (9,94 m); height, 13 ft 0 in (3,96 m); wing area, 229 sq ft (21,3 m²).

PIPER PA-34 SENECA

Country of Origin: USA.

Type: Light business executive transport.

Power Plant: Two 200 hp Lycoming IO-360-A1A four-cylinder horizontally-opposed engines.

Performance: Max. speed, 196 mph (316 km/h); max. cruise, 187 mph (301 km/h) at 6,000 ft (1 830 m); cruise at 65% power, 185 mph (298 km/h) at 9,000 ft (2 743 m), at 55% power, 180 mph (290 km/h) at 13,300 ft (4 054 m); range at 75% power, 860 mls (1 385 km), at 65% power, 960 mls (1 545 km), at 55% power, 1,070 mls (1 722 km), at 45% power, 1,160 mls (1 866 km); initial climb, 1,460 ft/min (7,42 m/sec); ceiling, 20,000 ft (6 096 m).

Weights: Empty equipped, 2,479 lb (1 124 kg); max. take-off, 4,000 lb (1 814 kg).

Accommodation: Standard accommodation for six persons in individual seats with alternative arrangement for seven persons with a three-across centre seat.

Status: Announced in September 1971 with deliveries commencing late same year.

Notes: The PA-34 Seneca is basically a twin-engined development of the single-engined PA-32 Cherokee Six, and is claimed by its manufacturer to be the lowest priced aircraft in its category. Emphasis has been placed on suitability for the twin-engined conversion training role.

PIPER PA-34 SENECA

Dimensions: Span, 38 ft 10¾ in (11,86 m); length, 28 ft 6 in (8,69 m); height, 9 ft 10¼ in (3,02 m); wing area, 206·5 sq ft (19,18 m²).

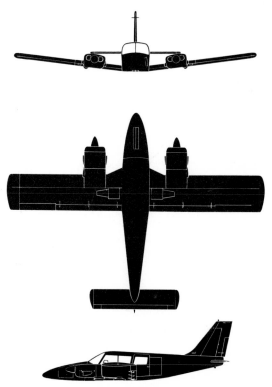

SAAB 35X DRAKEN

Country of Origin: Sweden.

Type: Single-seat multi-purpose fighter.

Power Plant: One 12,710 lb (5 765 kg) dry and 17,260 lb (7 830 kg) reheat Volvo Flygmotor RM 6C (Rolls-Royce RB 146 Mk. 60 Avon) turbojet.

Performance: Max. speed without external stores, 1,320 mph (2 125 km/h) or Mach 2·0 at 36,090 ft (11 000 m), with two 1,000-lb (453,5-kg) bombs and two 280 Imp gal (1 270 l) drop tanks, 925 mph (1 490 km/h) or Mach 1·4; tactical radius for hi-lo-hi mission profile without external fuel, 395 mls (635 km), with two 1,000-lb (453,5-kg) bombs and two 280 Imp gal (1 270 l) drop tanks, 620 mls (1 000 km); ferry range with four 280 Imp gal (1 270 l) drop tanks, 2,015 mls (3 245 km); initial climb, 34,450 ft/min (175 m/sec).

Weights: Loaded (clean aircraft), 25,130 lb (11 400 kg); max. take-off, 35,275 lb (16 000 kg).

Armament: Two 30-mm Aden M/55 cannon and up to 9,000 lb (4 082 kg) of ordnance distributed between nine external stations (six under wings and three under fuselage).

Status: Development airframe flown summer 1967, and first production Saab 35X (for Denmark) flown January 29, 1970.

Notes: The Saab 35X is an export version of the basic Draken (see Saab 35F, 1970 edition) ordered by Denmark and Finland. Denmark took delivery of the last of 40 single-seat Saab 35XDs (illustrated) and six two-seat Saab 35XTs late in 1971, and 12 single-seat Saab XSs have been ordered by Finland.

SAAB 35X DRAKEN

Dimensions: Span, 30 ft $10\frac{3}{4}$ in (9,40 m); length, 46 ft $10\frac{1}{4}$ in (14,28 m); height, 12 ft $8\frac{1}{3}$ in (3,89 m); wing area, 529·6 sq ft (49,2 m²).

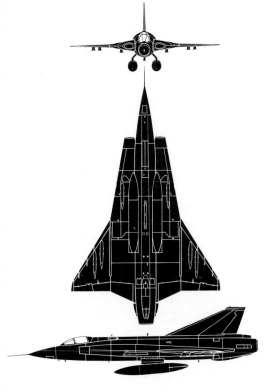

SAAB 37 VIGGEN

Country of Origin: Sweden.

Type: Single-seat multi-purpose fighter and two-seat operational trainer.

Power Plant: One 14,700 lb (6 667 kg) dry and 26,450 lb (12 000 kg) reheat Volvo Flygmotor RM 8 (Pratt & Whitney JT8D-22) turbofan.

Performance: (Estimated) Max. speed without external stores, 1,085 mph (1 745 km/h) or Mach 1·6 at 36,090 ft (11 000 m), 875 mph (1 410 km/h) or Mach 1·15 at 305 ft (100 m); tactical radius with typical external ordnance load for hi-lo-hi mission profile, 620 mls (1 000 km), for lo-lo-lo mission profile, 310 mls (500 km); time to 36,090 ft (11 000 m), 2 min.

Weights: Normal max. take-off, 35,275 lb (16 000 kg).

Armament: All ordnance carried on seven external stores stations (four beneath wings and three under fuselage), primary armament being RB 04C or RB 05A ASMs for the attack role, or RB 24 (Sidewinder), RB 27 or RB 28 (Falcon) AAMs for the intercept role.

Status: First of six single-seat prototypes flown February 8, 1967, and two-seat prototype of training version flown July 2, 1970. Orders placed by beginning of 1972 for 150 single-seat (AJ 37) and 25 two-seat (SK 37) Viggens. First production Viggen flown February 23, 1971, and deliveries to Swedish Air Force began June 21, 1971.

Notes: AJ 37 is primarily an attack aircraft with secondary intercept capability. Future versions include S 37 recce aircraft and JA 37 interceptor with variable intakes and Mach 2·0 performance.

194

SAAB 37 VIGGEN

Dimensions: Span, 34 ft 9¼ in (10,60 m); length, 50 ft 8¼ in (15,45 m), including probe, 53 ft 5¾ in (16,30 m); height, 18 ft 4½ in (5,60 m).

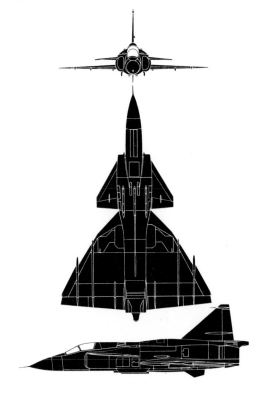

SAAB 105XT

Country of Origin: Sweden.

Type: Basic trainer and light strike and reconnaissance aircraft.

Power Plant: Two 2,850 lb (1 293 kg) General Electric J85-GE-17B turbojets.

Performance: Max. speed, 603 mph (970 km/h) at sea level, 543 mph (875 km/h) at 32,810 ft (10 000 m); range cruise, 435 mph (700 km/h) at 42,650 ft (13 000 m); range on internal fuel with 20 min reserves, 1,490 mls (2 400 km), with two 110 Imp gal (500 l) external tanks and 30 min reserves, 1,876 mls (3 020 km); tactical radius with six 500-lb (227-kg) bombs for hi-lo-hi mission profile, 514 mls (827 km), for lo-lo-lo mission profile, 200 mls (324 km).

Weights: Empty, 5,622 lb (2 550 kg); normal take-off, 9,822 lb (4 455 kg); max. take-off, 14,330 lb (6 500 kg).

Armament: Max. of 4,410 lb (2 000 kg) of ordnance distributed between six external wing stations.

Status: Prototype flown April 29, 1967, and first production deliveries (against order from Austria for 40) initiated July 1970.

Notes: The Saab 105XT is a more powerful, multi-purpose export version of the Saab 105 delivered to the Swedish Air Force (see 1968 edition) as the SK 60, this version having 1,640 lb (743 kg) Turboméca Aubisque turbofans. At the beginning of 1972 a further development of the export model, the Saab 105G, was being evolved, this having a semi-externally mounted 30-mm Aden cannon, 44 Imp gal (200 l) wingtip tanks, more advanced avionics, a modified wing, and larger air brakes.

SAAB 105XT

Dimensions: Span, 31 ft 2 in (9,50 m); length, 34 ft 5$\frac{1}{3}$ in (10,50 m); height, 8 ft 10$\frac{1}{4}$ in (2,70 m); wing area, 175·45 sq ft (16,3 m²).

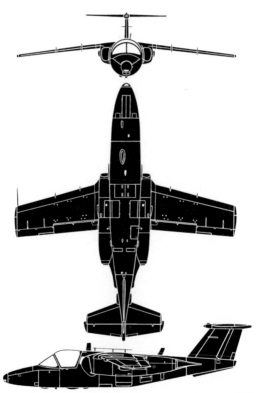

SCOTTISH AVIATION BULLDOG 100

Country of Origin: United Kingdom.

Type: Side-by-side two-seat primary trainer.

Power Plant: One 200 hp Lycoming IO-360-A1B6 four-cylinder horizontally-opposed engine.

Performance: Max. speed, 150 mph (240 km/h) at sea level; max. cruise, 138 mph (222 km/h) at 4,000 ft (1 220 m); econ. cruise, 121 mph (194 km/h) at 4,000 ft (1 220 m); max. range, 628 mls (1 010 km) at 4,000 ft (1 220 m); initial climb, 1,100 ft/min (5,58 m/sec); service ceiling, 17,000 ft (5 180 m).

Weights: Empty, 1,420 lb (644 kg); max. take-off, 2,350 lb (1 065 kg).

Status: Beagle-built first prototype flown May 19, 1969. Scottish Aviation-built definitive prototype flying on February 14, 1971, with first production aircraft following July 1971, production attaining six per month February 1972.

Notes: Originally designed by the now-liquidated Beagle Aircraft, the Bulldog was taken over by Scottish Aviation, which has developed the aircraft for production. Production orders have been placed for the Kenya (five aircraft), Royal Malaysian (15 aircraft) and Swedish (58 aircraft with an option on 25 more) air forces. The Swedish Army has ordered 20, and orders for some 130 for the RAF were expected early 1972. Scottish Aviation is investigating the possibility of introducing a high-lift slotted flap which, if successful, is likely to be fitted to those aircraft for the Swedish Army.

SCOTTISH AVIATION BULLDOG

Dimensions: Span, 33 ft 0 in (10,06 m); length, 23 ft 2½ in (7,07 m); height, 7 ft 5¾ in (2,28 m); wing area, 129·4 sq ft (12,02 m²).

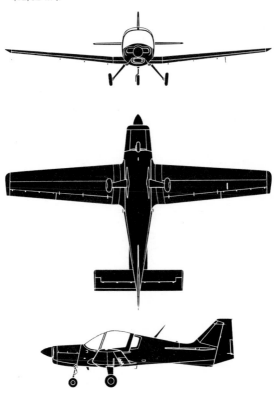

SEPECAT JAGUAR

Countries of Origin: France and United Kingdom.
Type: Single-seat tactical strike fighter and two-seat trainer.
Power Plant: Two 4,620 lb (2 100 kg) dry and 6,950 lb (3 150 kg) reheat Rolls-Royce Turboméca RB.172-T-260 Adour turbofans.
Performance: (Estimated) Max. speed, 820 mph (1 320 km/h) or Mach 1·1 at 1,000 ft (305 m), 1,130 mph (1 820 km/h) or Mach 1·7 at 32,810 ft (10 000 m); cruise with max. ordnance load, 430 mph (690 km/h) or Mach 0·65 at 39,370 ft (12 000 m); tactical radius on internal fuel with typical load for hi-lo-hi mission profile, 775 mls (1 250 km), for lo-lo-lo mission profile, 405 mls (650 km); ferry range with max. external fuel, 2,800 mls (4 500 km).
Weights: (Estimated) Empty, 14,990 lb (6 800 kg); normal take-off, 22,707 lb (10 300 kg); max. take-off, 29,762 lb (13 500 kg).
Armament: Two 30-mm Aden or DEFA 553 cannon and up to 10,000 lb (4 536 kg) ordnance on five external stores stations (one under fuselage and four under wings).
Status: First of eight prototypes flown September 8, 1968. Five versions being developed simultaneously and first production aircraft flown November 2, 1971.
Notes: Both France and UK have requirement for 200 Jaguars, French variants being the single-seat A (*Appui Tactique*), M (*Marine*) and two-seat E (*École de Combat*), and British versions being the single-seat S with laser range-finder in nose (illustrated) and two-seat B, the RAF being intended to receive 164 single-seaters and 36 two-seaters.

SEPECAT JAGUAR

Dimensions: Span, 27 ft 10¼ in (8,49 m); length, 50 ft 11 in (15,52 m); height, 16 ft 10 in (4,88 m); wing area, 258·33 sq ft (24 m²).

SHORT SKYVAN SERIES 3M

Country of Origin: United Kingdom.
Type: Light military utility transport.
Power Plant: Two 715 shp Garrett AiResearch TPE 331-201 turboprops.
Performance: Max. cruise, 201 mph (323 km/h) at 10,000 ft (3 050 m); econ. cruise, 173 mph (278 km/h) at 10,000 ft (3 050 m); range with max. fuel and 45 min reserves, 660 mls (1 062 km), with 5,000-lb (2 268-kg) payload and same reserves, 166 mls (267 km); initial climb, 1,520 ft/min (7,6 m/sec); service ceiling, 21,000 ft (6 400 m).
Weights: Basic operational, 7,400 lb (3 356 kg); max. take-off, 14,500 lb (6 577 kg).
Accommodation: Flight crew of one or two, and up to 22 fully-equipped troops, 16 paratroops and a despatcher, or 12 casualty stretchers and two medical attendants.
Status: Series 3M prototype flown early in 1970, and six delivered during course of year to Sultan of Oman's Air Force, this order being supplemented in 1971 by an order for a further two. Five ordered for Argentine Navy and two for Nepalese Army, another being ordered by the Ecuador Army. Interspersed on assembly line with civil Series 3, and combined production running at two per month at beginning of 1972 with some 65 ordered of both versions.
Notes: The Series 3M embodies features incorporated in two Skyvans supplied to the Austrian Air Force.

SHORT SKYVAN SERIES 3M

Dimensions: Span, 64 ft 11 in (19,79 m); length, 40 ft 1 in (12,21 m), with radome, 41 ft 4 in (12,60 m); height, 15 ft 1 in (4,60 m); wing area, 373 sq ft (34,65 m²).

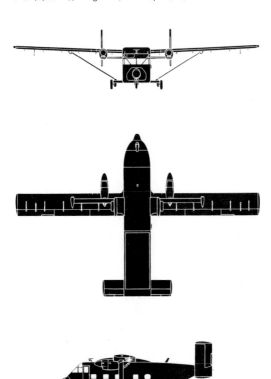

SIAI-MARCHETTI/FFA SA.202 BRAVO

Countries of Origin: Italy and Switzerland.
Type: Light training and touring monoplane.
Power Plant: One 150 hp Lycoming O-320-E2A four-cylinder horizontally-opposed engine.
Performance: (SA.202-15) Max. speed, 140 mph (225 km/h) at sea level; max. cruise, 130 mph (209 km/h); econ. cruise, 90 mph (145 km/h); range with max. fuel and no reserves, 685 mls (1 100 km); initial climb, 820 ft/min (4,16 m/sec); service ceiling, 13,000 ft (4 000 m).
Weights: Empty equipped, 1,336 lb (606 kg); max. take-off (aerobatic), 1,873 lb (850 kg), (utility), 2,204 lb (1 000 kg).
Accommodation: Two persons side-by-side with dual controls and optional aft seat for third person.
Status: Developed jointly by SIAI-Marchetti in Italy and FFA in Switzerland. First Swiss-built prototype flown March 7, 1969, and first Italian-built prototype flown May 7, 1969. First deliveries of SA.202-15 version were scheduled to commence late 1971 with production rate of 4–5 per month scheduled for May 1972.
Notes: Several variants of the Bravo are projected, the initial production version, the SA.202-15, being described above. The SA.202-10 (represented by the first Italian-built prototype) has a 115 hp Lycoming O-235-C2A, and a prototype with a 160 hp engine is proposed. SIAI-Marchetti produces the fuselage, tail and controls, and FFA the wings, undercarriage and engine installation.

SIAI-MARCHETTI/FFA SA.202 BRAVO

Dimensions: Span, 31 ft 9 in (9,78 m); length, 24 ft 6 in (7,55 m); height, 8 ft 3 in (2,52 m); wing area, 149 sq ft (13,86 m²).

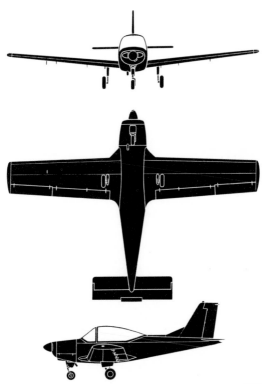

SIAI-MARCHETTI S.210

Country of Origin: Italy.

Type: Light cabin monoplane.

Power Plant: Two 200 hp Lycoming TIO-360-A1B four-cylinder horizontally-opposed engines.

Performance: Max. speed, 233 mph (375 km/h) at 18,700 ft (5 700 m); cruise at 75% power, 215 mph (346 km/h) at 18,700 ft (5 700 m); max. range, 1,180 mls (1 190 km); initial climb, 1,560 ft/min (7,92 m/sec).

Weights: Empty equipped, 2,359 lb (1 070 kg); max. take-off, 4,078 lb (1 850 kg).

Accommodation: Pilot and five passengers in three pairs of side-by-side seats.

Status: First of two prototypes flown February 18, 1970, and work initiated on pre-production series of 10 airframes during course of 1971.

Notes: A twin-engined derivative of the S.205–S.208 range of single-engined light cabin monoplanes and possessing extensive structural component commonality with its predecessors, the S.210 has been under development for several years, prototype trials being delayed by the priority attached to establishing the company's single-engined line. The second prototype differs from that illustrated above in having staggered entry doors (rear port, front starboard), an enlarged baggage compartment door, and enlarged rear windows. A military version, the S.210M, is under development.

SIAI-MARCHETTI S.210

Dimensions: Span, 38 ft 2 in (11,63 m); length, 28 ft 11$\frac{7}{8}$ in (8,83 m); height, 10 ft 1$\frac{3}{4}$ in (3,09 m); wing area, 185·5 sq ft (17,23 m²).

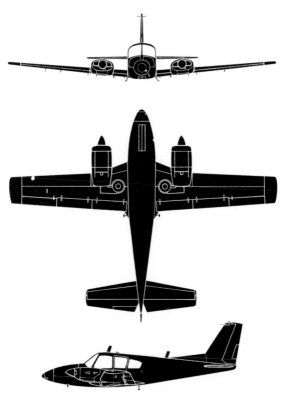

SIAI-MARCHETTI SF.260MX

Country of Origin: Italy.
Type: Primary training monoplane.
Power Plant: One 260 hp Lycoming O-540-E4A5 six-cylinder horizontally-opposed engine.
Performance: Max. speed, 230 mph (370 km/h) at sea level; max. cruise, 214 mph (345 km/h) at 10,000 ft (3 050 m); econ. cruise, 203 mph (327 km/h) at 10,000 ft (3 050 m); max. range (with two persons), 1,275 mls (2 050 km); initial climb, 1,770 ft/min (10 m/sec); service ceiling, 21,370 ft (6 500 m).
Weights: Empty (standard equipment), 1,543 lb (700 kg); max. loaded (aerobatic), 2,205 lb (1 000 kg); max. take-off, 2,650 lb (1 200 kg).
Accommodation: Two side-by-side seats with full dual controls, and aft bench normally occupied by one person.
Status: SF.260MX is the generic designation for the export military version of the SF.260 cabin monoplane originally developed by Aviamilano. Deliveries commenced 1970.
Notes: Essentially similar apart from equipment to the civil SF.260, this aircraft has been selected as an elementary trainer by the air arms of four countries, Belgium having ordered 36 (as SF.260MBs), the Republic of Zaire (Congo) having ordered 12 (as SF.260MCs) and taken an option on a further 12, Zambia having ordered eight (as SF.260MZs), and Singapore having ordered 16 (as SF.260MSs).

208

SIAI-MARCHETTI SF.260MX

Dimensions: Span, 26 ft 11¾ in (8,25 m); length, 23 ft 0 in (7,02 m); height, 8 ft 6 in (2,60 m); wing area, 108·5 sq ft (10,1 m²).

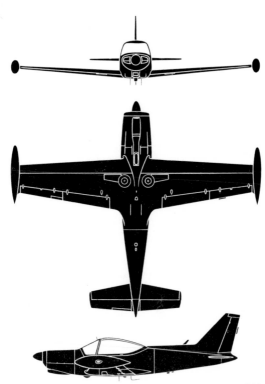

SIAI-MARCHETTI SM.1019A

Country of Origin: Italy.

Type: Battlefield surveillance and forward air control aircraft.

Power Plant: One 317 shp Allison 250-B15G turboprop.

Performance: Max. speed, 188 mph (302 km/h) at 6,000 ft (1 830 m); max. cruise, 173 mph (278 km/h) at 6,000 ft (1 830 m); econ. cruise, 135 mph (217 km/h) at 10,000 ft (3 050 m); range with max. fuel and 10 min reserves, 765 mls (1 230 km), with 500-lb (227-kg) external stores on wing stations and same reserves, 320 mls (515 km); initial climb, 1,625 ft (8,25 m/sec).

Weights: Empty equipped, 1,480 lb (672 kg); max. take-off, 2,513 lb (1 140 kg).

Armament: Two stores stations under wings capable of carrying minigun pods, rockets, etc., up to a maximum external load of 500 lb (227 kg).

Status: First of two prototypes flown May 24, 1969 and second on July 14, 1970. A production line for 100 aircraft was being laid down late 1971.

Notes: The SM.1019 is based upon the Cessna O-1 Bird Dog but possesses an extensively modified airframe to meet latest operational requirements, redesigned tail surfaces, and a turboprop in place of the O-1's piston engine. The second prototype, the SM.1019A, has a second door for the observer and duplicated instrument panel. At the end of 1971 the SM.1019 was competing with the AM.3C (see pages 6–7) for a production order for the Italian Army, and was unofficially reported as the chosen type, the placing of an order for 100 examples being anticipated.

SIAI-MARCHETTI SM.1019A

Dimensions: Span, 36 ft 0 in (10,97 m); length, 27 ft 8 in (8,43 m); height, 7 ft 9¾ in (2,38 m); wing area, 173·94 sq ft (16,16 m²).

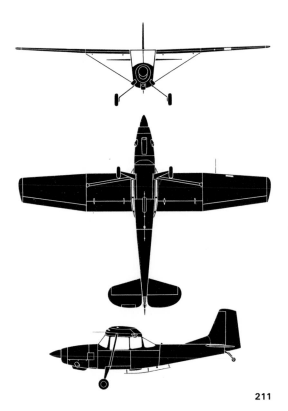

SUKHOI SU-7MF (FITTER)

Country of Origin: USSR.

Type: Single-seat ground attack fighter.

Power Plant: One (approx.) 22,050 lb (10 000 kg) reheat Lyulka AL-7F-1 turbojet.

Performance: (Estimated) Max. speed without external stores, 720 mph (1 160 km/h) or Mach 0·95 at 1,000 ft (305 m), 1,056 mph (1 700 km/h) at 39,370 ft (12 000 m), in high-drag configuration (e.g. two rocket pods and two 132 Imp gal/600 l drop tanks), 790 mph (1 270 km/h) or Mach 1·2 at 39,370 ft (12 000 m); combat radius for hi-lo-hi mission profile, 285 mls (460 km); initial climb without external stores, 29,500 ft/min (150 m/sec).

Weights: (Estimated) Normal take-off, 26,455 lb (12 000 kg); max. take-off, 30,865 lb (14 000 kg).

Armament: Two 30-mm NR-30 cannon and such loads as two 550-lb (250-kg) bombs and two UV-16-57 pods each containing 16 55-mm rockets distributed between four external stores stations (two under wings and two under fuselage).

Status: Prototypes allegedly flown 1955 with production deliveries of initial service version to the Soviet Air Forces commencing 1958.

Notes: The Su-7 has been widely exported, the latest single-seat production model reportedly being the Su-7MF with up-rated engine and improved short-field characteristics. A tandem two-seat conversion trainer variant, the Su-7UTI, dubbed Moujik by NATO (see 1970 edition) is also in service.

212

SUKHOI SU-7MF (FITTER)

Dimensions: (Estimated) Span, 31 ft 2 in (9,50 m); length, 55 ft 9 in (17,00 m); height, 15 ft 5 in (4,70 m).

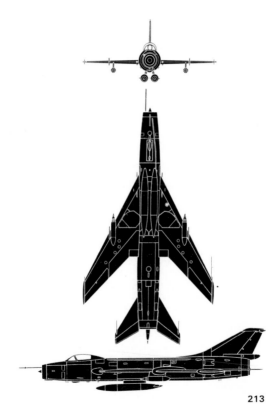

213

SUKHOI SU-11 (FLAGON-A)

Country of Origin: USSR.

Type: Single-seat all-weather interceptor fighter.

Power Plant: Two (approx.) 25,000 lb (11 340 kg) reheat Lyulka AL-9 turbojets.

Performance: (Estimated) Max. speed without external stores, 1,650 mph (2 655 km/h) or Mach 2·5 at 39,370 ft (12 000 m), 910 mph (1 465 km/h) or Mach 1·2 at 1,000 ft (305 m), with AAMs on wing stations and twin drop tanks on fuselage stations, 1,120 mph (1 800 km/h) or Mach 1·7 at 39,370 ft (12 000 m); range at subsonic cruise with max. external fuel, 1,500 mls (2 415 km).

Weights: (Estimated) Normal take-off, 50,000–55,000 lb (22 680–24 950 kg).

Armament: Basic armament for intercept mission reportedly comprises two AAMs of Anab type on wing stations, but various ordnance loads may be carried for the attack role, these being distributed between two fuselage and two wing stations.

Status: The Su-11 is believed to have flown in prototype form during 1964–65 with production deliveries commencing 1967.

Notes: Apparently optimised for the intercept role as a successor to the Su-9 (see 1969 edition), the Su-11 is in large-scale service with the Soviet Air Forces. A STOL version with direct lift engines, the Flagon-B, is illustrated above but is of uncertain status.

SUKHOI SU-11 (FLAGON-A)

Dimensions: (Estimated) Span, 31 ft 3 in (9,50 m); length, 70 ft 6 in (21,50 m); height, 16 ft 6 in (5,00 m).

215

TRANSALL C. 160

Countries of Origin: France and Federal Germany.
Type: Medium-range tactical transport.
Power Plant: Two 5,665 shp Rolls-Royce Tyne R.Ty. 20 Mk. 22 turboprops.
Performance: Max. speed, 333 mph (536 km/h) at 14,765 ft (4 500 m); max. cruise, 319 mph (513 km/h) at 18,045 ft (5 500 m); range with 17,640-lb (8 000–kg) payload and reserves of 10% plus 30 min hold, 2,832 mls (4 558 km), with 35,270-lb (16 000-kg) payload and same reserves, 730 mls (1 175 km); initial climb, 1,440 ft/min (7,3 m/sec); service ceiling at 99,225 lb (45 000 kg), 27,900 ft (8 500 m).
Weights: Empty equipped, 63,400 lb (28 758 kg); normal take-off, 97,450 lb (44 200 kg); max. take-off, 108,250 lb (49 100 kg).
Accommodation: Flight crew of four and 93 troops, 81 paratroops, or 62 casualty stretchers and four medical attendants. Other possible loads include armoured vehicles not exceeding 35,270 lb (16 000 kg) total weight.
Status: First of three prototypes flown February 25, 1963, and first of six pre-production aircraft flown on May 21, 1965. Total orders for 169 production aircraft comprising 50 for France (C. 160F), 110 for Federal Germany (C. 160D), and nine for South Africa (C. 160Z), production being scheduled to phase out in 1972.
Notes: VFW-Fokker is overall Transall project manager, other participants being MBB and Aérospatiale. Sixteen C.160Ds surplus to Federal German requirements are being transferred to the Turkish Air Force, the first of these being delivered in June 1971.

TRANSALL C. 160

Dimensions: Span, 131 ft 2½ in (40,00 m); length, 106 ft 3½ in (32,40 m); height, 38 ft 4¾ in (11,65 m); wing area, 1,722·7 sq ft (160,1 m²).

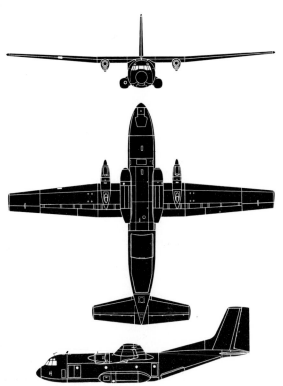

TRANSAVIA PL-12-U AIRTRUK

Country of Origin: Australia.

Type: Light agricultural and utility aircraft.

Power Plant: One 300 hp Continental IO-520-D six-cylinder horizontally-opposed engine.

Performance: Max. speed, 129 mph (208 km/h) at sea level; max. cruise (75% power), 117 mph (188 km/h) at sea level; range with max. payload, 748 mls (1 203 km), with max. fuel, 806 mls (1 297 km); initial climb, 800 ft/min (4,06 m/sec); service ceiling, 10,500 ft (3 200 m).

Weights: Empty equipped, 1,830 lb (830 kg); max. take-off, 3,800 lb (1 723 kg).

Accommodation: Single-seat cockpit for pilot, four passengers on lower deck, and a fifth passenger on upper deck if chemical tank/hopper removed.

Status: Prototype Airtruk flown April 22, 1965, with deliveries of production PL-12 version commencing December 1966. Prototype of PL-12-U version flown December 1970 with production deliveries commencing during 1971.

Notes: The Airtruk was originally designed specifically for the agricultural role, and the PL-12-U model is basically similar to the original PL-12 apart from some revision of the fuselage pod design. Some 60 Airtruks of both versions had been delivered to customers in Australia, New Zealand, Kenya, South Africa and elsewhere by the beginning of 1972 when consideration was being given by the manufacturer to a twin-float version and to an armed variant suitable for close-support operations.

218

TRANSAVIA PL-12-U AIRTRUK

Dimensions: Span, 39 ft 10½ in (12,15 m); length, 20 ft 10 in (6,35 m); height, 9 ft 2 in (2,79 m); wing area, 252·7 sq ft (23,48 m²).

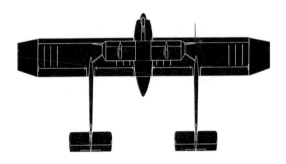

TUPOLEV TU-22 (BLINDER)

Country of Origin: USSR.

Type: Long-range medium bomber and strike-reconnaissance aircraft.

Power Plant: Two (approx.) 27,000 lb (12 250 kg) reheat turbojets.

Performance: (Estimated) Max. speed without external stores, 990 mph (1 590 km/h) or Mach 1·5 at 39,370 ft (12 000 m), 720 mph (1 160 km/h) or Mach 0·95 at 1,000 ft (305 m); normal cruise, 595 mph (960 km/h) or Mach 0·9 at 39,370 ft (12 000 m); tactical radius on standard fuel for high-altitude mission, 700 mls (1 125 km); service ceiling, 60,000 ft (18 290 m).

Weights: (Estimated) Max. take-off, 185,000 lb (84 000 kg).

Armament: Free-falling weapons housed internally or (Blinder-B) semi-recessed Kitchen ASM. Remotely-controlled 23-mm cannon in tail barbette.

Status: Believed to have attained operational status with the Soviet Air Forces in 1965.

Notes: The Tu-22 is the successor to the subsonic Tu-16 in Soviet medium-bomber formations and with shore-based maritime strike elements of the Soviet Naval Air Arm. The basic version, dubbed Blinder-A by NATO, is illustrated above, the missile-carrying Blinder-B being illustrated on the opposite page. A training version, the Blinder-C (see 1970 edition), features a raised second cockpit for the instructor. Recent production models of the Tu-22 display a number of modifications, including an extended flight refuelling probe and enlarged engine air intakes, nacelles and exhaust orifices.

TUPOLEV TU-22 (BLINDER)

Dimensions: (Estimated) Span, 91 ft 0 in (27,74 m); length, 133 ft 0 in (40,50 m); height, 17 ft 0 in (5,18 m); wing area, 2,030 sq ft (188,59 m²).

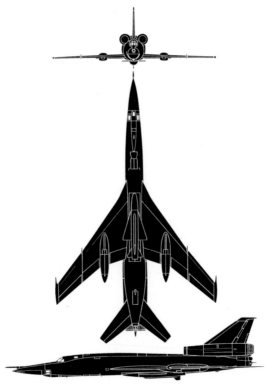

TUPOLEV TU-28P (FIDDLER)

Country of Origin: USSR.

Type: Two-seat long-range all-weather interceptor and reconnaissance-strike aircraft.

Power Plant: Two (approx.) 24,250 lb reheat turbojets.

Performance: (Estimated) Max. speed without external stores, 1,085 mph (1 745 km/h) or Mach 1·65 at 39,370 ft (12 000 m), with four Ash AAMs on wing stores stations, 925 mph (1 490 km/h) or Mach 1·4 at 39,370 ft (12 000 m); tactical radius for high-altitude patrol mission, 900–1,100 mls (1 450–1 770 km).

Weights: (Estimated) normal take-off, 78,000 lb (35 380 kg); max. take-off, 96,000 lb (43 545 kg).

Armament: Four infra-red or radar-homing Ash AAMs on wing stations for intercept role.

Status: The Tu-28 is believed to have flown in prototype form in 1957 and to have entered service in its Tu-28P interceptor version during the early 'sixties.

Notes: The Tu-28 is believed to have been evolved originally to fulfil a requirement for a long-range reconnaissance-strike aircraft, and its design was biased towards economical high-altitude operation. It serves in some numbers with the Soviet Air Forces primarily for patrolling the sections of the periphery of the Soviet Union unprotected by surface-to-air missile screens, and there is currently no western equivalent of this warplane. One version has been seen with a central pack that may be presumed to house early warning radar, and it is probable that an internal weapons bay is standard for the reconnaissance-strike role.

TUPOLEV TU-28P (FIDDLER)

Dimensions: (Estimated) Span, 65 ft 0 in (19,80 m); length, 90 ft 0 in (27,43 m).

TUPOLEV TU-134A (CRUSTY)

Country of Origin: USSR.

Type: Short- to medium-range commercial transport.

Power Plant: Two 14,990 lb (6 800 kg) Soloviev D-30-2 Turbofans.

Performance: Max. cruise, 528 mph (850 km/h) at 32,810 ft (10 000 m); long-range cruise, 466 mph (750 km/h) at 32,810 ft (10 000 m); max. range at long-range cruise with 1 hr reserves and 18,108-lb (8 215-kg) payload, 1,243 mls (2 000 km), with 8,818-lb (4 000-kg) payload, 2,175 mls (3 500 km).

Weights: Operational empty, 63,934 lb (29 000 kg); max. take-off, 103,617 lb (47 000 kg).

Accommodation: Basic flight crew of three and maximum of 80 passengers in four-abreast all-tourist class configuration.

Status: Prototype Tu-134A flown in 1968 and first production deliveries (to *Aeroflot*) mid-1970.

Notes: The Tu-134A differs from the original Tu-134, which entered *Aeroflot* service in 1966, in having an additional 6 ft 10⅔ in (2,10 m) section inserted in the fuselage immediately forward of the wing to permit two additional rows of passenger seats, and introduces engine thrust reversers. Maximum take-off weight has been increased by 5,512 lb (2 500 kg), maximum payload being raised by 1,025 lb (465 kg), an APU is provided, and radio and navigational equipment have been revised. Route proving trials with the Tu-134A were completed by *Aeroflot* late in 1970, and this airliner was introduced on international routes early in 1971. The shorter-fuselage Tu-134 (illustrated above) serves with CSA, Interflug, LOT, Malev, United Arab, Balkan-Bulgarian and Aviogenex.

TUPOLEV TU-134A (CRUSTY)

Dimensions: Span, 95 ft 2 in (29,00 m); length, 111 ft 0½ in (36,40 m); height, 29 ft 7 in (9,02 m); wing area, 1,370·3 sq ft (127,3 m²).

TUPOLEV TU-144 (CHARGER)

Country of Origin: USSR.
Type: Long-range supersonic commercial transport.
Power Plant: Four 28,660 lb (13 000 kg) dry and 38,580 lb (17 500 kg) Kuznetsov NK-144 turbofans.
Performance: (Estimated) Max. cruise, 1,550 mph (2 500 km/h) or Mach 2·35 between 49,200 and 65,600 ft (15 000 and 20 000 m); range with max. payload, 4,040 mls (6 500 km).
Weights: Max. take-off, 286,600 lb (130 000 kg).
Accommodation: Basic flight crew of three, and mixed-class arrangement for 82 tourist-class and 18 first-class passengers, or all-tourist arrangement for 121 passengers.
Status: First prototype commenced flight test programme on December 31, 1968. First of two production prototypes joined the development programme during September 1971, and initial batch of 14 production aircraft reportedly under construction at beginning of 1972.
Notes: The Tu-144 possesses the distinction of having been the world's first commercial transport to exceed both Mach 1·0 (on June 5, 1969) and Mach 2·0 (on May 26, 1970), reaching 1,336 mph (2 150 km/h), or Mach 2·02, at 53,500 ft (16 300 m) during the latter flight. Like the competitive Anglo-French Concorde (see pages 42–43), the Tu-144 employs an ogival delta wing, a retractable vizor for cruising flight, and a droopable nose for take-off and landing. It is intended that the Tu-144 be used on one-stop trans-Siberian services, and on some external services, including the Moscow–Delhi and Moscow–New York runs commencing 1973–74.

TUPOLEV TU-144 (CHARGER)

Dimensions: (Prototypes) Span, 90 ft 8½ in (27,65 m); length (excluding probe), 194 ft 10½ in (59,40 m).

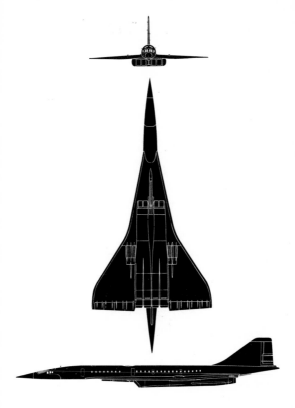

TUPOLEV TU-154 (CARELESS)

Country of Origin: USSR.

Type: Medium- to long-range commercial transport.

Power Plant: Three 20,950 lb (9 500 kg) Kuznetsov NK-8-2 turbofans.

Performance: Max. cruise, 605 mph (975 km/h) at 31,170 ft (9 500 m); long-range cruise, 528 mph (850 km/h) at 37,730 ft (11 500 m); range with standard fuel and reserves of 1 hr plus 6% and max. payload, 2,150 mls (3 460 km) at 560 mph (900 km/h), 2,360 mls (3 800 km) at 528 mph (850 km/h).

Weights: Operational empty, 95,900 lb (43 500 kg); normal take-off, 185,188 lb (84 000 kg); max. take-off, 198,416 lb (90 000 kg).

Accommodation: Basic flight crew of three–four, and alternative arrangements for 158 or 150 economy-class passengers, 150, 146 or 136 tourist-class passengers, or 24 first-class and 104 tourist-class passengers.

Status: First prototype flown October 4, 1968, with first delivery of a production aircraft (to *Aeroflot*) following August 1970, route proving commencing August 1971.

Notes: The Tu-154 was scheduled to enter service on *Aeroflot* routes early 1972, is intended as a successor to the Tu-104, Il-18 and An-10 on medium- to long-range routes, and can operate from airfields with category B surfaces, including packed earth and gravel. A growth version, referred to as the Tu-154M, is currently under development with flight testing scheduled for 1972. This model will incorporate additional fuselage sections which will enable 220–240 passengers to be accommodated, and will have uprated NK-8 turbofans.

TUPOLEV TU-154 (CARELESS)

Dimensions: Span, 123 ft 2½ in (37,55 m); length, 157 ft 1¾ in (47,90 m); height, 37 ft 4¾ in (11,40 m); wing area, 2,168·92 sq ft (201,45 m²).

VFW-FOKKER VAK 191B

Country of Origin: Federal Germany.

Type: Experimental single-seat V/STOL reconnaissance and strike fighter.

Power Plant: One 10,207 lb (4 630 kg) Rolls-Royce/MTU RB. 193-12 vectored-thrust turbojet and two 5,578 lb (2 530 kg) Rolls-Royce/MTU RB. 162-81 lift turbojets.

Performance: (Estimated) Max. speed, 730 mph (1 175 km/h) or Mach 0·96 at 1,000 ft (305 m), 605 mph (975 km/h) or Mach 0·92 at 39,370 ft (12 000 m).

Weights: Empty equipped, 11,695 lb (5 305 kg); max. (vertical) take-off, 17,626 lb (7 995 kg).

Status: First untethered flight trials of the first prototype initiated on September 10, 1971, followed by the second prototype on October 2, 1971, and all three prototypes were expected to be participating in the test programme by early 1972.

Notes: The VAK 191B was originally designed to meet an Italo-German requirement for a subsonic VTOL tactical reconnaissance fighter which was discarded as a result of changes in German strategy. With completion of the exploration of the flight envelope of the VAK 191B, the prototypes will be transferred by the manufacturer to the German Government for use as systems test vehicles for the Panavia multi-role combat aircraft (MRCA), evaluating avionic components and flight control elements. VFW-Fokker is currently proposing a Mk. 2 production version with an enlarged wing of 24 ft 7¼ in (7,50 m) span and 204·5 sq ft (19,0 m²) area.

VFW-FOKKER VAK 191B

Dimensions: Span, 20 ft 2½ in (6,16 m); length, 48 ft 3½ in (14,72 m); height, 14 ft 1 in (4,29 m); wing area, 134·5 sq ft (12,5 m²).

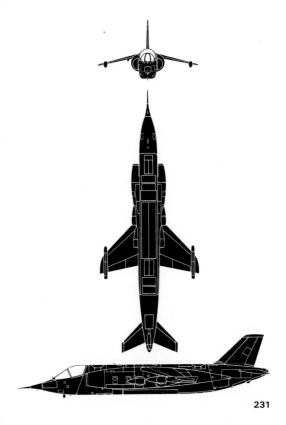

VFW-FOKKER VFW 614

Country of Origin: Federal Germany.

Type: Short-range commercial transport.

Power Plant: Two 7,510 (3 410 kg) Rolls-Royce/SNECMA M45H turbofans.

Performance: (Estimated) Max. speed, 457 mph (735 km/h) at 21,000 ft (6 400 m); max. cruise, 449 mph (722 km/h) at 25,000 ft (7 620 m); long-range cruise, 390 mph (627 km/h) at 25,000 ft (7 620 m); range with max. fuel, 1,145 mls (1 845 km), with max. payload. 390 mls (630 km); initial climb rate, 3,248 ft min (16,5 m/sec).

Weights: Operational empty, 26,896 lb (12 000 kg); max. take-off, 41,006 lb (18 600 kg).

Accommodation: Basic flight crew of two and alternative passenger configurations for 36, 40 or 44 seats in four-abreast rows.

Status: First of three prototypes commenced its flight test programme on June 14, 1971, and second was rolled out on December 8, 1971. First production aircraft scheduled to be completed August 1972.

Notes: The VFW 614 is being manufactured as a collaborative venture under the leadership of VFW-Fokker, participants including the Dutch Fokker-VFW concern and the Belgian SABCA and Fairey companies. The VFW 614 is intended as an ultra-short-haul DC-3 replacement, and an unconventional feature is its over-wing engine-pod installation. Emphasis has been placed on flexibility of operation in a wide variety of different environments and with a minimum of maintenance.

VFW-FOKKER VFW 614

Dimensions: Span, 70 ft 6½ in (21,50 m); length, 67 ft 7 in (20,60 m); height, 25 ft 8 in (7,84 m); wing area, 688·89 sq ft (64,00 m²).

VOUGHT A-7E CORSAIR II

Country of Origin: USA.

Type: Single-seat shipboard tactical fighter.

Power Plant: One 15,000 lb (6 804 kg) Allison TF41-A-2 (Rolls-Royce RB. 168-62 Spey) turbofan.

Performance: Max. speed without external stores, 699 mph (1 125 km/h) or Mach 0·92 at sea level, with 12 250-lb (113,4-kg) bombs, 633 mph (1 020 km/h) or Mach 0·87 at sea level; tactical radius with 12 250-lb (113,4-kg) bombs for hi-lo-hi mission at average cruise of 532 mph (856 km/h) with 1 hr on station, 512 mls (825 km); ferry range on internal fuel, 2,775 mls (4 465 km).

Weights: Empty equipped, 17,569 lb (7 969 kg); max. take-off, 42,000+ lb (19 050+ kg).

Armament: One 20-mm M-61A-1 rotary cannon with 1,000 rounds and (for short-range interdiction) maximum ordnance load of 20,000 lb (9 072 kg) distributed between eight external stores stations.

Status: A-7E first flown November 25, 1968, with production deliveries to US Navy following mid-1969. First 67 delivered with Pratt & Whitney TF30-P-8 turbofan. Planned procurement totals 618 aircraft.

Notes: A-7E is the shipboard equivalent of the USAF's A-7D (see 1970 edition). Preceded into service by A-7A (199 built) and A-7B (196 built) with 11,350 lb (5 150 kg) TF30-P-6 and 12,200 lb (5 534 kg) TF30-P-8 respectively. The A-7G is a proposed version for the Swiss Air Force with an uprated TF41-A-3 turbofan, and a supersonic version with a TF30-P-408 and afterburner has been proposed for USMC use.

VOUGHT A-7E CORSAIR II

Dimensions: Span, 38 ft 8¾ in (11,80 m); length, 46 ft 1½ in (14,06 m); height, 16 ft 0¾ in (4,90 m); wing area, 375 sq ft (34,83 m²).

WASSMER WA-43 GUÉPARD

Country of Origin: France.
Type: Light cabin monoplane.
Power Plant: One 250 hp Lycoming IO-540 six-cylinder horizontally-opposed engine.
Performance: Max. speed, 199 mph (320 km/h) at sea level; max. cruise at 75% power, 193 mph (310 km/h) at 6,560 ft (2 000 m); max. range, 1,740 mls (2 800 km); service ceiling, 16,400 ft (5 000 m).
Weights: Empty equipped, 1,863 lb (845 kg); max. take-off, 3,130 lb (1 420 kg).
Accommodation: Basic seating capacity for four persons with two individual seats in front and rear bench seat.
Status: Prototype first flown on May 18, 1971, with production deliveries scheduled to commence in 1972.
Notes: The Guépard (Cheetah), initially announced as the CERVA-43, is basically an all-metal derivative of the mixed-construction Wassmer WA 4/21 (see 1968 edition) which was continuing in production at the beginning of 1972. The Guépard retains the general features of its predecessor, and embodies electrically-retractable undercarriage and electrically-operated flaps. By comparison with the WA 4/21, the Guépard features some aerodynamic refinement and is claimed to be particularly suitable for the basic training role, and at the time of closing for press was to be evaluated for possible use by the École de l'Air de Salon-de-Provence.

WASSMER WA-43 GUÉPARD

Dimensions: Span, 32 ft 9½ in (10,00 m); length, 25 ft 7 in (7,80 m); height, 9 ft 5 in (2,86 m); wing area, 172·22 sq ft (16,0 m²).

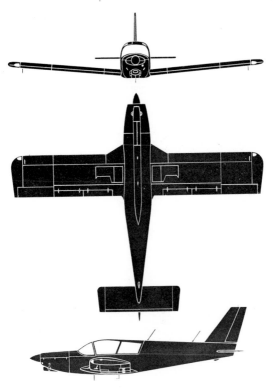

WINDECKER AC-7 EAGLE 1

Country of Origin: USA.

Type: Light cabin monoplane.

Power Plant: One 285 hp Continental IO-520-C six-cylinder horizontally-opposed engine.

Performance: Max. speed, 211 mph (340 km/h) at sea level; max. cruise, 204 mph (328 km/h) at 7,000 ft (2 135 m); econ. cruise, 202 mph (325 km/h) at 12,000 ft (3 658 m); range with max. fuel and 45 min reserves, 1,230 mls (1 980 km) at 10,000 ft (3 050 m); initial climb, 1,220 ft/min (6,2 m/sec); service ceiling, 18,000 ft (5 486 m).

Weights: Empty equipped, 2,150 lb (975 kg); max. take-off, 3,400 lb (1 542 kg).

Accommodation: Four persons in pairs.

Status: First prototype flown January 26, 1969, and second following on September 29, 1969, with first production aircraft being delivered on October 7, 1970.

Notes: The AC-7 Eagle 1 has the distinction of being the first aircraft manufactured of glass-fibre reinforced plastic to attain production. Resulting from a research programme initiated in 1958 by Doctors L. J. and F. M. Windecker, the Eagle is of conventional configuration but is of monocoque construction, and meets strength factors 20% higher than those of comparable metal aircraft.

WINDECKER AC-7 EAGLE 1

Dimensions: Span, 32 ft 0 in (9,75 m); length, 28 ft 5 in (8,66 m); height, 9 ft 5 in (2,87 m); wing area, 167 sq ft (15,51 m²).

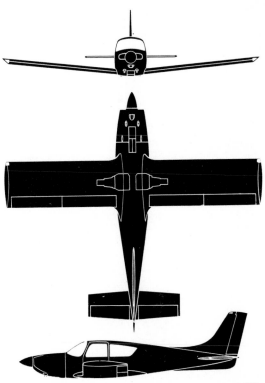

YAKOVLEV YAK-28P (FIREBAR)

Country of Origin: USSR.

Type: Two-seat all-weather interceptor fighter.

Power Plant: Two 10,140 lb (4 600 kg) dry and 13,670 lb (6 200 kg) reheat Tumansky RD-11 turbojets.

Performance: (Estimated) Max. speed without external stores, 760 mph (1 225 km/h) or Mach 1·15 at 39,370 ft (12 000 m), with two Anab AAMs, 695 mph (1 120 km/h) or Mach 1·05; normal cruise, 560 mph (900 km/h) or Mach 0·9; tactical radius for high-altitude patrol mission, 550 mls (885 km); initial climb, 28,000 ft/min (142,2 m/sec); service ceiling, 55,000 ft (16 765 m).

Weights: (Estimated) Normal take-off, 37,480 lb (17 000 kg); max. take-off, 40,785 lb (18 500 kg).

Armament: Standard armament comprises two Anab semi-active radar-homing AAMs carried by stores stations under wing. Some examples have been seen with four wing stores stations for two Anab AAMs and two infra-red homing Atoll AAMs.

Status: Flown in prototype form in 1960 with production deliveries commencing 1963–64.

Notes: The Yak-28P was developed in parallel with the Yak-28 tactical strike-recce aircraft, featuring a dielectric nose cone, tandem seating for the two crew members with windscreen (and twin-wheel forward member of "bicycle" undercarriage) about 2 ft 6 in (76 cm) further forward, and internal weapons bay deleted, this space presumably being occupied by fuel tankage. The Yak-28P is widely used by the Soviet Air Forces.

240

YAKOVLEV YAK-28P (FIREBAR)

Dimensions: (Estimated) Span, 44 ft 6 in (13,56 m); length (with probe), 75 ft 0 in (22,86 m), (without probe), 67 ft 0 in (20,42 m); height, 15 ft 0 in (4,57 m).

YAKOVLEV YAK-28U (MAESTRO)

Country of Origin: USSR.

Type: Advanced operational conversion trainer.

Power Plant: Two 10,140 lb (4 600 kg) dry and 13,670 lb (6 200 kg) reheat Tumansky R-11 turbojets.

Performance: (Estimated) Max. speed, 720 mph (1 160 km/h) or Mach 0·95 at 1,000 ft (305 m), 730 mph (1 175 km/h) or Mach 1·1 at 39,370 ft (12 000 m); tactical radius with two 220 Imp gal (1 000 l) drop tanks, 490 mls (790 km).

Weights: (Estimated) Normal take-off, 37,480 lb (17 000 kg); max. take-off, 41,890 lb (19 000 kg).

Armament: One 30-mm NR-30 cannon on starboard side of forward fuselage. Internal weapons bay believed to accommodate four 551-lb (250-kg) bombs.

Status: Derivative of the Yak-28 (*Brewer*) tactical strike and reconnaissance aircraft, the Yak-28U entered service in the mid 'sixties.

Notes: The Yak-28U is an adaptation of the early production Yak-28, and differs primarily from the later Yak-28 (see 1971 edition) in having a shorter fuselage. The internal weapons bay is retained but the glazed nose is deleted.

YAKOVLEV YAK-28U (MAESTRO)

Dimensions: (Estimated) Span, 44 ft 6 in (13,56 m); length (with probe), 72 ft 6 in (22,10 m), (without probe), 64 ft 6 in (19,66 m); height, 15 ft 0 in (4,57 m).

YAKOVLEV YAK-40 (CODLING)

Country of Origin: USSR.

Type: Short-range commercial feederliner.

Power Plant: Three 3,307 lb (1 500 kg) Ivchenko AI-25 turbofans.

Performance: Max. speed, 373 mph (600 km/h) at sea level, 466 mph (750 km/h) at 17,000 ft (5 180 m); max. cruise, 342 mph (550 km/h) at 19,685 ft (6 000 m); econ. cruise, 310 mph (500 km/h) at 32,810 ft (10 000 m); range with 5,070-lb (2 300-kg) payload at econ. cruise, 620 mls (1 000 km), with 3,140-lb (1 425-kg) payload and max. fuel, 920 mls (1 480 km); initial climb, 2,000 ft/min (10,16 m/sec); service ceiling at max. loaded weight, 38,715 ft (11 800 m).

Weights: Empty equipped, 19,865–21,715 lb (9 010–9 850 kg); normal take-off, 27,250–34,170 lb (12 360–15 500 kg); max. take-off, 36,375 lb (16 500 kg).

Accommodation: Flight crew of two, and alternative arrangements for 27 or 34 passengers in three-abreast rows. High-density arrangement for 40 passengers in four-abreast rows, and business executive configuration for 8–10 passengers.

Status: First of five prototypes flown October 21, 1966, and first production deliveries (to *Aeroflot*) mid-1968. Some 360 delivered by beginning of 1972.

Notes: A thrust reverser introduced as standard on centre engine during 1971 when more powerful version with three 3,858 lb (1 750 kg) AI-25T turbofans and increased fuel capacity announced for 1972 delivery.

244

YAKOVLEV YAK-40 (CODLING)

Dimensions: Span, 82 ft 0¼ in (25,00 m); length, 66 ft 9½ in (20,36 m); height, 21 ft 4 in (6,50 m); wing area, 753·473 sq ft (70 m²).

AÉROSPATIALE SA 318C ALOUETTE II

Country of Origin: France.

Type: Five-seat light utility helicopter.

Power Plant: One 523 shp Turboméca Astazou IIA turbo-shaft.

Performance: Max. speed, 127 mph (205 km/h) at sea level; max. cruise, 112 mph (180 km/h); max. inclined climb, 1,396 ft/min (7, 1 m/sec); hovering ceiling (in ground effect), 5,085 ft (1 550 m), (out of ground effect), 2,950 ft (900 m); range with max. fuel, 447 mls (720 km), with max. payload, 62 mls (100 km).

Weights: Empty, 1,961 lb (890 kg); max. take-off, 3,630 lb (1 650 kg).

Dimensions: Rotor diam, 33 ft 5$\frac{5}{8}$ in (10,20 m); fuselage length, 31 ft 11$\frac{3}{4}$ in (9,75 m).

Notes: The SA 318C has been developed from the SE 313B Alouette II (see 1967 edition) which it has supplanted in production. The earlier model differed primarily in having an Artouste turboshaft, and 923 examples were built. The Astazou offers a 25 per cent improvement in fuel consumption and, together with other design changes, has provided the SA 318C version of the Alouette II with performance improvements and a 375-lb (170-kg) increase in payload. The SA 315B Lama is a version of the Alouette II with an Artouste IIB and mechanical systems of the Alouette III certificated in September 1970.

AÉROSPATIALE SA 319A ALOUETTE III

Country of Origin: France.
Type: Seven-seat light utility helicopter.
Power Plant: One 789 shp Turboméca Astazou XIV turboshaft.
Performance: Max. speed, 137 mph (220 km/h) at sea level; max. cruise, 122 mph (197 km/h); max. inclined climb, 853 ft/min (4,32 m/sec); hovering ceiling (in ground effect), 5,740 ft (1 750 m); range with six passengers, 375 mls (605 km).
Weights: Empty, 2,403 lb (1 090 kg); max. take-off, 4,960 lb (2 250 kg).
Dimensions: Rotor diam, 36 ft 1¾ in (11,02 m); fuselage length, 32 ft 10¾ in (10,03 m).
Notes: The SA 319 is an Astazou-powered derivative of the Artouste-powered SA 316 Alouette III. All Alouette IIIs built prior to 1970 had the Artouste turboshaft and are now designated SA316A, the 1970 production model with the Artouste IIIB of 858 shp derated to 543 shp being the SA 316B, and the 1971 model with the Artouste IIID being the SA 316C. The last-mentioned version is manufactured in parallel with the SA 319A, deliveries of which began late in 1970, and the SA 319B with the Astazou XVI was introduced in 1971. A total of 988 Alouette IIIs ordered by the beginning of 1972, and licence production being undertaken in India, Switzerland, and Rumania.

AÉROSPATIALE SA 321 SUPER FRELON

Country of Origin: France.
Type: Medium transport and multi-purpose helicopter.
Power Plant: Three 1,550 shp Turboméca Turmo III C6 turboshafts.
Performance: Max. speed, 149 mph (240 km/h) at sea level; max. cruise, 143 mph (230 km/h); max. inclined climb, 1,495 ft/min (7,6 m/sec); hovering ceiling (in ground effect), 7,380 ft (2 250 m), (out of ground effect), 1,804 ft (550 m); range with 5,511-lb (2 500-kg) payload and 20 min reserves, 404 mls (650 km).
Weights: Empty, 14,420 lb (6 540 kg); max. take-off, 27,557 lb (12 500 kg).
Dimensions: Rotor diam, 62 ft 0 in (18,90 m); fuselage length, 63 ft 7¾ in (19,40 m).
Notes: Several versions of the Super Frelon (Super Hornet) have been manufactured, including the SA 321G amphibious ASW model for the *Aéronavale* (illustrated above) with Sylph radars in outrigger floats, dunking sonar and up to four torpedoes and other ASW stores, the non-amphibious military transport SA 321K (Israel) and SA 321L (South Africa) capable of carrying 27–30 troops or 8,818–9,920 lb (4 000–4 500 kg) cargo, and the commercial SA 321F (34–37 passenger airliner) and SA 321J heavy-duty utility models. A total of 57 SA 321s ordered by beginning of 1972.

AÉROSPATIALE SA 330 PUMA

Country of Origin: France.
Type: Medium transport helicopter.
Power Plant: Two 1,320 shp Turboméca Turmo III C4 turbo-shafts.
Performance: Max. Speed, 174 mph (280 km/h) at sea level; max. cruise, 165 mph (265 km/h); max. inclined climb, 1,400 ft/min (7,1 m/sec); hovering ceiling (in ground effect), 9,186 ft (2 800 m), (out of ground effect), 6,233 ft (1 900 m); max. range, 390 mls (630 km).
Weights: Empty, 7,561 lb (3 430 kg); max. take-off, 14,110 (6 400 kg).
Dimensions: Rotor diam, 49 ft 2½ on (15,00 m), fuselage length, 46 ft 1½ in (14,06 m).
Notes: The Puma is being built under a joint production agreement between Aérospatiale and Westland, the first to be assembled by the latter concern flying on November 25, 1970. The Puma can accommodate 16–20 troops or up to 5,511 lb (2 500 kg) of cargo, and 40 are being delivered to the RAF for the assault role, 88 having been ordered by French Army Aviation. The Puma has been supplied to the Portuguese, South African, Zaire Rep., Algerian, and Ivory Coast air arms, and a commercial version, the SA 330F with 1,385 shp Turmo IVA turboshafts, obtained FAA Type Approval in 1971, this carrying 15–17 passengers over 217 mls (350 km).

AÉROSPATIALE SA 341 GAZELLE

Country of Origin: France.
Type: Five-seat light utility helicopter.
Power Plant: One 592 shp Turboméca Astazou IIIN turbo-shaft.
Performance: Max. speed, 165 mph (265 km/h) at sea level; max. cruise, 149 mph (240 km/h); max. inclined climb rate, 1,214 ft/min (6,16 m/sec); hovering ceiling (in ground effect), 10,170 ft (3 100 m), (out of ground effect), 8,530 ft (2 600 m); max. range, 403 mls (650 km).
Weights: Empty, 1,873 lb (850 kg); max. take-off, 3,747 lb (1 700 kg).
Dimensions: Rotor diam, 34 ft 5½ in (10,50 m); fuselage length, 31 ft 2¾ in (9,52 m).
Notes: Intended as a successor to the Alouette II, the Gazelle is being built under a joint production agreement between Aérospatiale and Westland. Two prototypes and four pre-production Gazelles have flown, and the first production example flew on August 6, 1971. The Gazelle is to be operated in the LOH (Light Observation Helicopter) role by both the French and British armed forces, and it is anticipated that these will respectively purchase some 170 and 250 Gazelles during the first half of the decade. Licence production is to be undertaken in Yugoslavia with deliveries commencing in 1973.

AGUSTA A 109C HIRUNDO

Country of Origin: Italy.

Type: Eight-seat utility helicopter.

Power Plant: Two 400 shp Allison 250-C20 turboshafts.

Performance: (At 4,850 lb/2 200 kg) Max. speed, 169 mph (272 km/h) at sea level; econ. cruise, 139 mph (223 km/h) at sea level; max. inclined climb, 2,067 ft/min (10,5 m/sec); hovering ceiling (in ground effect), 11,810 ft (3 600 m), (out of ground effect), 9,190 ft (2 800 m); max. range, 457 mls (735 km) at 6,560 ft (2 000 m).

Weights: Empty, 2,645 lb (1 200 kg); max. take-off, 5,291 lb (2 400 kg).

Dimensions: Rotor diam, 36 ft 1 in (11,00 m); fuselage length, 36 ft 7 in (11,14 m).

Notes: The first of four Hirundo (Swallow) prototypes flew on August 4, 1971, and the first production examples are scheduled to be delivered late 1972. The Hirundo is intended to fit between the licence-built Bell 206 JetRanger and Bell 212 in the Agusta helicopter range, and carries a pilot and seven passengers in its basic form. It is also suitable for the ambulance role, accommodating two casualty stretchers and two medical attendants when the forward cabin bulkhead is removed, and for freight carrying the forward row of passenger seats may be removed.

BELL MODEL 204B (IROQUOIS)

Country of Origin: USA.

Type: Ten-seat utility helicopter.

Power Plant: One 1,100 shp Lycoming T5311A turboshaft.

Performance: (At 8,500 lb/3 855 kg) Max. speed, 120 mph (193 km/h) at sea level; max. cruise, 110 mph (177 km/h); max. inclined climb, 1,400 ft/min (7,1 m/sec); hovering ceiling (in ground effect), 10,000 ft (3 050 m), (out of ground effect), 4,500 ft (1 370 m); max. range, 392 mls (630 km).

Weights: Empty, 4,600 lb (2 086 kg); max. take-off, 9,500 lb (4 309 kg).

Dimensions: Rotor diam, 48 ft 0 in (14,63 m); fuselage length 40 ft 4⅞ in (12,31 m).

Notes: Licence manufacture of Model 204B undertaken in Italy by Agusta (as AB 204B) and in Japan by Fuji. Variants for US forces include UH-1B and -1C (two crew and seven troops) for US Army, UH-1E (assault support equivalent of of the UH-1C) for the USMC, the UH-1F (missile-site support model with a 1,272 shp General Electric T58-GE-3) and TH-1F (trainer) for the USAF, and the HH-1K (sea-rescue version of the UH-1E with a 1,400 shp Lycoming T53 L-13), TH-1L Seawolf (T53-L-13-powered trainer), and the UH-1L (utility version of the TH-1L) for the US Navy. The AB-204B may have the Gnome H.1200 or T58-GE-3 turboshaft.

BELL MODEL 205A (IROQUOIS)

Country of Origin: USA.

Type: Fifteen-seat utility helicopter.

Power Plant: One 1,400 shp Lycoming T5313A turboshaft.

Performance: (At 9,500 lb/4 309 kg) Max. speed, 127 mph (204 km/h) at sea level; max. cruise, 111 mph (179 km/h) at 8,000 ft (2 440 m); max. inclined climb, 1,680 ft/min (8,53 m/sec); hovering ceiling (in ground effect), 10,400 ft (3 170 m), (out of ground effect), 6,000 ft (1 830 m); range, 344 mls (553 km) at 8,000 ft (2 440 m).

Weights: Empty equipped, 5,082 lb (2 305 kg); normal take-off, 9,500 lb (4 309 kg).

Dimensions: Rotor diam, 48 ft 0 in (14,63 m); fuselage length, 41 ft 6 in (12,65 m).

Notes: The Model 205A is basically similar to the Model 204B but introduces a longer fuselage with increased cabin space. It is produced under licence in Italy by Agusta as the AB 205, and is assembled under licence in Formosa (Taiwan). The initial version for the US Army, the UH-1D, has a 1,100 shp T53-L-11 turboshaft. This model was manufactured under licence in Federal Germany. The UH-1D has been succeeded in production for the US Army by the UH-1H (illustrated) with a 1,400 shp T53-L-13 turboshaft, and a similar helicopter for the Mobile Command of the Canadian Armed Forces is designated CUH-1H.

BELL MODEL 206A JETRANGER

Country of Origin: USA.
Type: Five-seat light utility helicopter.
Power Plant: One 317 shp Allison 250-C18A turboshaft.
Performance: Max. speed, 150 mph (241 km/h) at sea level; max. cruise, 131 mph (211 km/h); max. inclined climb at 3,000 lb (1 360 kg), 1,450 ft/min (7,36 m/sec); hovering ceiling (in ground effect), 7,900 ft (2 410 m), (out of ground effect), 3,350 ft (1 020 m); max. range at 2,100 lb (953 kg), 460 mls (740 km), at 3,000 lb (1 360 kg), 392 mls (630 km).
Weights: Empty, 1,425 lb (646 kg); max. take-off, 3,000 lb (1 360 kg).
Dimensions: Rotor diam, 33 ft 4 in (10,16 m); fuselage length, 31 ft 2 in (9,50 m).
Notes: The Model 206A JetRanger is manufactured in both commercial and military versions. Forty have been delivered to the US Navy for the training role as the TH-57A Sea-Ranger, and a light observation version is being produced for the US Army as the OH-58A Kiowa. The latter differs from the basic Model 206A in having a larger main rotor of 35 ft 4 in (10,77 m) diameter, a fuselage of 32 ft 3½ in (9,84 m) length, and other changes. A version of the JetRanger basically similar to the OH-58A is built in Italy by Agusta as the AB 206A-1, and has been exported in some numbers for both civil and military use.

BELL MODEL 209 HUEYCOBRA

Country of Origin: USA.
Type: Two-seat attack helicopter.
Power Plant: (AH-1G) One 1,400 shp Lycoming T53-L-13 turboshaft.
Performance: (AH-1G) Max. speed, 219 mph (352 km/h) at sea level; max. inclined climb, 1,580 ft/min (8 m/sec); hovering ceiling (in ground effect), 9,900 ft (3 015 m); max. range, 387 mls (622 km) at sea level.
Weights: Operational empty, 6,096 lb (2 765 kg); max. take-off, 9,500 lb (4 309 kg).
Dimensions: Rotor diam, 44 ft 0 in (13,41 m); fuselage length, 44 ft 5 in (13,54 m).
Notes: The Model 209 is a development of the UH-1C version of the Model 204B (see page 252) specifically for armed missions. The version for the US Army, the AH-1G (described and illustrated above), has two 7,62-mm Miniguns with 4,000 rpg or two 40-mm grenade launchers with 300 rpg in a forward barbette, and four external stores stations for rockets or gun pods under the stub-wings. The variant for the USMC, the AH-1J SeaCobra, differs from the AH-1G in having a 1,800 shp Pratt & Whitney T400-CP-400 coupled free-turbine turboshaft, a three-barrel 20-mm cannon in the chin barbette, a strengthened tail rotor pylon, and a maximum take-off weight of 10,000 lb (4 535 kg). SeaCobra deliveries commenced mid-1970.

255

BELL MODEL 212 TWIN TWO-TWELVE

Country of Origin: USA.
Type: Fifteen-seat utility helicopter.
Power Plant: One 1,800 shp Pratt & Whitney PT6T-3 coupled turboshaft.
Performance: Max. speed, 121 mph (194 km/h) at sea level; max. inclined climb at 10,000 lb (4 535 kg), 1,460 ft/min (7,4 m/sec); hovering ceiling (in ground effect), 17,100 ft (5 212 m), (out of ground effect), 9,900 ft (3 020 m); max. range, 296 mls (476 km) at sea level.
Weights: Empty, 5,500 lb (2 495 kg); max. take-off, 10,000 lb (4 535 kg).
Dimensions: Rotor diam, 48 ft 2$\frac{1}{2}$ in (14,69 m); fuselage length, 42 ft 10$\frac{3}{4}$ in (13,07 m).
Notes: The Model 212 is based on the Model 205 (see page 253) from which it differs primarily in having a twin-engined power plant (two turboshaft engines coupled to a combining gearbox with a single output shaft), and both commercial and military versions are being produced. A model for the Canadian Armed Forces (illustrated) is designated CUH-1N, and an essentially similar variant of the Model 212, the UH-1N, is being supplied to the USAF, the USN, and the USMC. All versions of the Model 212 can carry an external load of 4,400 lb (1 814 kg), and can maintain cruise performance on one engine component at maximum gross weight.

BELL MODEL 309 KINGCOBRA

Country of Origin: USA.
Type: Two-seat attack helicopter.
Power Plant: One 1,800 shp Pratt & Whitney T400-CP-400 coupled turboshaft.
Performance: Approx. max. speed, 230 mph (370 km/h); hovering ceiling (out of ground effect), 4,000 ft (1 220 m).
Weights: Max. take-off, 14,000 lb (6 350 kg).
Dimensions: Rotor diam, 49 ft 0 in (14,93 m); fuselage length, 49 ft 0 in (14,93 m).
Notes: The KingCobra is a company-funded development, the first prototype with a T400-CP-400 coupled turboshaft having first flown on September 10, 1971. A second prototype powered by a single 2,850 shp Lycoming T55-L-7C turboshaft was scheduled to commence its test programme early in 1972. The KingCobra is essentially a growth version of the Model 209 (see page 255) with substantially more power, an enlarged fuselage and a rotor of new design. The first prototype, illustrated above, is fitted with a General Electric chin barbette which can mount either a 20-mm or 30-mm rotary cannon, and the 13-ft (3,96-m) span fixed wing embodies four hardpoints for weapons pylons, a typical underwing load comprising four Hughes TOW missiles and 19 2·75-in (70-mm) rockets beneath each wing. Infra-red, low-light-level television and laser systems are mounted in the nose.

BOEING-VERTOL MODEL 107-II

Country of Origin: USA.

Type: Medium transport helicopter.

Power Plant: Two 1,500 shp General Electric T58-GE-5 turboshafts.

Performance: (At 20,800 lb/9 434 kg) Max. speed, 139 mph (224 km/h); max. inclined climb, 1,920 ft/min (9,75 m/sec); hovering ceiling (in ground effect), 10,000 ft (3 048 m), (out of ground effect), 7,100 ft (2 165 m); range with 2,400 lb (1 088 kg) payload and 30 min reserves, 633 mls (1 020 km).

Weights: Empty equipped, 11,585 lb (5 240 kg); max. take-off, 21,400 lb (9 706 kg).

Dimensions: Rotor diam (each), 50 ft 0 in (15,24 m); fuselage length, 44 ft 10 in (13,66 m).

Notes: The Model 107-II has been in continuous production for military and civil tasks for 11 years, and is licence-manufactured by Kawasaki in Japan for the Air, Ground and Maritime Self-Defence Forces. The specification relates to the latest basic utility model. Versions supplied to the US services comprise the CH-46A (1,250 shp T58-GE-8Bs), CH-46D (1,400 shp T58-GE-10s) and CH-46F (additional electronics) Sea Knight assault transports for the USMC, and the similarly-powered UH-46A (illustrated) and UH-46D Sea Knight utility models for the US Navy. The Model 107-II accommodates three crew and 25 passengers.

BOEING-VERTOL MODEL 114

Country of Origin: USA.

Type: Medium transport helicopter.

Power Plant: (CH-47C) Two 3,750 shp Lycoming T55-L-11 turboshafts.

Performance: (CH-47C at 33,000 lb/14 969 kg) Max. speed, 190 mph (306 km/h) at sea level; average cruise, 158 mph (254 km/h); max. inclined climb, 2,880 ft/min (14,63 m/sec); hovering ceiling (out of ground effect), 14,750 ft (4 495 m); mission radius, 115 mls (185 km).

Weights: Empty, 20,378 lb (9 243); max. take-off, 46,000 lb (20 865 kg).

Dimensions: Rotor diam (each), 60 ft 0 in (18,29 m); fuselage length, 51 ft 0 in (15,54 m).

Notes: The Model 114 is the standard medium transport helicopter of the US Army, and is operated by that service under the designation CH-47 Chinook. The initial production model, the CH-47A, was powered by 2,200 shp T55-L-5 or 2,650 shp T55-L-7 turboshafts. This was succeeded by the CH-47B with 2,850 shp T55-L-7C engines, redesigned rotor blades and other modifications, and this, in turn, gave place to the current CH-47C with more powerful engines, strengthened transmissions, and increased fuel capacity. This model is manufactured in Italy by Elicotteri Meriodionali, orders calling for 26 for the Italian Army and 16 for the Iranian Army (illustrated).

EMA 124

Country of Origin: Italy.

Type: Three-seat light utility helicopter.

Power Plant: One 305 hp (derated to 250 shp) Lycoming VO-540-B1B3 six-cylinder horizontally-opposed engine.

Performance: Max. speed, 106 mph (170 km/h) at sea level; cruise, 90 mph (145 km/h) at sea level; inclined climb, 827 ft/min (4,2 m/sec); hovering ceiling (in ground effect), 8,200 ft (2 500 m), (out of ground effect), 5,575 ft (1 700 m); max. range, 260 mls (420 km).

Weights: Empty, 1,543 lb (700 kg); max. take-off, 2,535 lb (1 150 kg).

Dimensions: Rotor diam, 31 ft 2 in (9,50 m).

Notes: The EMA 124 has been designed by Costruzioni Aeronautiche Giovanni Agusta for Elicotteri Meriodionali which is to manufacture the type under a licence agreement, the two companies sharing the development work. The EMA 124 is expected to enter production during the course of 1972, and has a two-blade semi-rigid main rotor with provision for blade folding. Derived by Agusta from the Bell 47 series helicopters which it is intended to replace, the EMA 124 is suitable for pilot training, survey, reconnaissance, casualty evacuation, and general policing tasks. The flight test programme of the EMA 124 was initiated in 1970, and had been virtually completed by the beginning of 1972 when production plans were being finalised.

FAIRCHILD 1100

Country of Origin: USA.

Type: Five-seat light utility helicopter.

Power Plant: One 317 shp Allison 250-C18 turboshaft.

Performance: Max. speed, 127 mph (204 km/h) at sea level; econ. cruise, 122 mph (196 km/h); max. inclined climb, 1,600 ft/min (8,1 m/sec); hovering ceiling (in ground effect), 13,400 ft (4 085 m), (out of ground effect), 8,400 ft (2 560 m); range with max. payload, 348 mls (560 km).

Weights: Empty, 1,396 lb (633 kg); max. take-off, 2,750 lb (1 247 kg).

Dimensions: Rotor diam, 35 ft $4\frac{3}{4}$ in (10,79 m); fuselage length, 29 ft $9\frac{1}{2}$ in (9,08 m).

Notes: The Model 1100 is a refined derivative of the OH-5A which was runner-up in the US Army's first light observation helicopter contest, and the first production model was completed in June 1966. The Model 1100 has since been manufactured in some numbers, primarily for civil duties, and an aeromedical version provides accommodation for two casualty stretchers and a medical attendant. The Model 1100 serves with the Thai Royal Border Police, and is suitable for a variety of military roles. Provision can be made for a wide range of weapons, including torpedoes, depth charges, minigun pods, and rocket launchers, and the Model 1100 has been flown in level flight at 160 mph (257 km/h).

HUGHES MODEL 300

Country of Origin: USA.

Type: Three-seat light utility helicopter.

Power Plant: (Model 300C) One 190 shp Lycoming HIO-360-D1A four-cylinder horizontally-opposed engine.

Performance: (Model 300C) Max. speed, 105 mph (169 km/h); max. cruise, 100 mph (161 km/h) at 5,000 ft (1 525 m); max. inclined climb, 1,100 ft/min (5,08 m/sec); hovering ceiling (in ground effect), 7,600 ft (2 316 m), (out of ground effect), 5,200 ft (1 585 m); max. range, 255 mls (410 km).

Weights: Empty, 1,025 lb (465 kg); max. take-off, 1,900 lb (861 kg).

Dimensions: Rotor diam, 26 ft 10 in (8,18 m); fuselage length, 23 ft 1 in (7,03 m).

Notes: Originally developed as the Model 269B, the Model 300 has been in continuous production since 1963, and 792 examples of this light helicopter have been supplied to the US Army for the primary training role as the TH-55A. The current production version, the Model 300C described by the specification, differs from the basic Model 300 (which was powered by a 180 hp Lycoming HIO-360-A1A) in having a more powerful engine, main and tail rotors of increased diameter, and structural changes including a lengthened tail boom and a taller rotor mast. Deliveries of the Model 300C commenced in 1970.

HUGHES MODEL 500

Country of Origin: USA.

Type: Six-seat light utility helicopter.

Power Plant: One 317 shp Allison 250-C18A turboshaft.

Performance: Max. speed, 152 mph (244 km/h) at 1,000 ft (305 m); range cruise, 138 mph (222 km/h) at sea level; max. inclined climb, 1,700 ft/min (8,64 m/sec); hovering ceiling (in ground effect), 8,200 ft (2 500 m), (out of ground effect), 5,300 ft (1 615 m); max. range, 377 mls (589 km) at 4,000 ft (1 220 m).

Weights: Empty, 1,086 lb (492 kg); max. take-off, 2,550 lb (1 157 kg).

Dimensions: Rotor diam, 26 ft 4 in (8,03 m); fuselage length, 23 ft 0 in (7,01 m).

Notes: The Model 500 (also known by the engineering designation Model 369) is being manufactured for both commercial and foreign military use, the military configuration being known as the Model 500M. Both Models 500 and 500M have been assembled in Italy by Nardi which began licence manufacture during 1971, and licence manufacture is also being undertaken by Kawasaki in Japan. The current Model 500 is essentially similar to the OH-6A Cayuse light observation helicopter for the US Army, but its turboshaft is only derated to 278 shp (as compared with 252 shp for the Allison T63-A-5A of the OH-6A), and internal volume and fuel capacity are increased.

KAMAN HH-2 SEASPRITE

Country of Origin: USA.
Type: All-weather search and rescue helicopter.
Power Plant: Two 1,250 shp General Electric T58-GE-8B turboshafts.
Performace: (HH-2D) Max. speed, 168 mph (270 km/h) at sea level; normal cruise, 152 mph (245 km/h); max. inclined climb, 2,540 ft/min (12,9 m/sec); hovering ceiling (in ground effect), 16,900 ft (5 150 m), (out of ground effect), 14,100 ft (4 300 m); max. range, 425 mls (685 km).
Weights: (HH-2D) Empty, 7,500 lb (3 401 kg); normal take-off, 10,187 lb (4 620 kg); max. overload, 12,500 lb (5 670 kg).
Dimensions: Rotor diam, 44 ft 0 in (13,41 m); fuselage length, 37 ft 8 in (11,48 m).
Notes: The HH-2C and HH-2D are specialised search and rescue conversions of the single-engined UH-2A and -2B multi-role versions of the Seasprite (see 1966 edition), and, like the UH-2C (see 1969 edition), are modified to twin-engined configuration. The HH-2C is an armed and armoured model with a chin-mounted Minigun barbette and waist-mounted machine guns, and the HH-2D is similar but lacks armour and armament. The HH-2D differs from the UH-2C in having a four-bladed tail rotor, dual main-wheels, and uprated transmission, and the SH-2D (illustrated) is an adaptation for anti-submarine warfare and missile defence.

KAMOV KA-25 (HORMONE A)

Country of Origin: USSR.

Type: Shipboard anti-submarine warfare helicopter.

Power Plant: Two 900 shp Glushenkov GTD-3 turboshafts.

Performance: (Ka-25K) Max. speed, 137 mph (220 km/h); normal cruise, 121 mph (195 km/h); range with max. payload, 248 mls (400 km), with max. fuel, 404 mls (650 km); service ceiling, 10,670 ft (3 500 m).

Weights: (Ka-25K) Empty, 9,259 lb (4 200 kg); normal take-off, 15,653 lb (7 100 kg); max. take-off, 16,094 lb (7 300 kg).

Dimensions: Rotor diam (each), 51 ft 7½ in (15,74 m); fuselage length, 34 ft 3 in (10,44 m).

Notes: Developed to meet a requirement for a shipboard ASW helicopter, the Ka-25 was initially flown in prototype form in 1961, and was subsequently developed for both military and civil roles, the civil version, the Ka-25K (see 1970 edition), being flown in prototype form in 1965. The ASW Ka-25, which serves aboard the helicopter carriers *Moskva* and *Leningrad*, and the Ka-25K possess the same power plant, transmission system, and coaxial contra-rotating rotors, but the latter has a slightly shorter fuselage (32 ft 3 in/9,83 m), and aft-facing glazed gondola beneath the nose to accommodate a winch operator, and smaller vertical tail surfaces. The ASW Ka-25 is equipped with inflatable pontoons.

KAMOV KA-26 (HOODLUM)

Country of Origin: USSR.

Type: Light utility helicopter.

Power Plant: Two 325 shp Vedeneev M-14V-26 air-cooled radial engines.

Performance: Max. speed, 106 mph (170 km/h); max. cruise, 93 mph (150 km/h); econ. cruise, 56 mph (90 km/h) at 9,840 ft (3 000 m); hovering ceiling at 6,615 lb (3 000 kg) (in ground effect), 4,265 ft (1 300 m), (out of ground effect), 2,625 ft (800 m); range with seven passengers and 30 min reserves, 248 mls (400 km).

Weights: Empty (stripped), 4,300 lb (1 950 kg), (with passenger pod), 4,630 lb (2 100 kg); max. take-off, 7,165 lb (3 250 kg).

Dimensions: Rotor diam (each), 42 ft 8 in (13,00 m); fuselage length, 25 ft 5 in (7,75 m).

Notes: Flown for the first time in 1965, and placed in large-scale production during the following year, the Ka-26 was designed from the outset to carry interchangeable pods for freight or passengers, a chemical hopper with spraybars or dust-spreader, an open freight platform, or a hook for slung loads. The passenger-carrying pod (see fitted above) can accommodate up to six passengers, and in the aero-medical role the Ka-26 can carry two casualty stretchers, two seated casualties and a medical attendant.

MBB BO 105

Country of Origin: Federal Germany.
Type: Five/six-seat light utility helicopter.
Power Plant: Two 400 shp Allison 250-C20 turboshafts.
Performance: Max. speed, 155 mph (250 km/h) at sea level; max. cruise, 138 mph (222 km/h); max. inclined climb, 1,870 ft/min (9,5 m/sec); hovering ceiling (in ground effect), 7,610 ft (2 320 m), (out of ground effect), 5,085 ft (1 550 m); normal range, 388 mls (625 km) at 5,000 ft (1 525 m).
Weights: Empty, 2,360 lb (1 070 kg); normal take-off, 4,630 lb (2 100 kg); max. take-off, 5,070 lb (2 300 kg).
Dimensions: Rotor diam, 32 ft 1¾ in (9,80 m); fuselage length, 28 ft 0½ in (8,55 m).
Notes: The BO 105 features a rigid unarticulated main rotor with folding glass-fibre reinforced plastic blades, and the first prototype (with a conventional rotor) was tested in 1966, three prototypes being followed by four pre-production examples, and production deliveries commencing during 1971. The German armed forces are acquiring six examples for evaluation, and US manufacturing rights have been acquired by Boeing Vertol. The third prototype was powered by 375 shp MTU 6022 turboshafts, but the production model has standardised on the Allison 250. Production is undertaken by the Siebelwerke-ATG subsidiary of MBB.

MIL MI-2 (HOPLITE)

Country of Origin: USSR.
Type: Light general-purpose helicopter.
Power Plant: Two 437 shp Izotov GTD-350 turboshafts.
Performance: Max. speed, 130 mph (210 km/h) at 1,640 ft (500 m); max. cruise, 124 mph (200 km/h); econ. cruise, 118 mph (190 km/h); max. inclined climb, 885 ft/min (4,5 m/sec); hovering ceiling (in ground effect), 6,550 ft (2 000 m), (out of ground effect), 3,275 ft (1 000 m); range with max. payload and 5% reserves, 105 mls (170 km), with max. fuel and 30 min reserves, 360 mls (580 km).
Weights: Operational empty, 5,180 lb (2 350 kg); normal take-off, 7,826 lb (3 550 kg); overload take-off, 8,157 lb (3 700 kg).
Dimensions: Rotor diam, 47 ft $6\frac{3}{4}$ in (14,50 m); fuselage length, 37 ft $4\frac{3}{4}$ in (11,40 m).
Notes: After completion of prototype development in the Soviet Union, production and marketing of the Mi-2 were transferred to Poland where manufacture of this helicopter (at the WSK-Swidnik) has been undertaken since 1966. The Mi-2 has been built in large numbers for both civil and military tasks, and has been exported widely. Accommodation may be provided for a single pilot and six to eight passengers or up to 1,543 lb (700 kg) of freight. Four casualty stretchers and a medical attendant can be carried.

MIL MI-6 (HOOK)

Country of Origin: USSR.
Type: Heavy transport helicopter.
Power Plant: Two 5,500 shp Soloviev D-25V turboshafts.
Performance: (At 93,700 lb/42 500 kg) Max. speed, 186 mph (300 km/h); max. cruise, 155 mph (250 km/h); service ceiling, 14,750 ft (4 500 m); range with 17,640-lb (8 000-kg) payload, 385 mls (620 km), with 9,920-lb (4 500-kg) payload and external tanks, 620 mls (1 000 km).
Weights: Empty, 60,055 lb (27 240 kg); normal take-off, 89,285 lb (40 500 kg); max. take-off (for VTO), 93,700 lb (42 500 kg).
Dimensions: Rotor diam, 114 ft 10 in (35,00 m); fuselage length, 108 ft 9½ in (33,16 m).
Notes: First flown in 1957, the Mi-6 has been built in very large numbers for both civil and military roles. With a crew of five, the Mi-6 can accommodate 65 passengers or 41 casualty stretchers and two medical attendants, and clam-shell-type doors and folding ramps facilitate the loading of vehicles and bulky freight. Two heavy flying-crane helicopters have been evolved from the Mi-6, the Mi-10 (see 1966 edition) flown in 1961 and the Mi-10K (see 1970 edition) flown in 1965, these being almost identical to the Mi-6 above the line of the cabin. The Mi-6 has been supplied to the armed forces of North Vietnam, UAR and Indonesia.

MIL MI-8 (HIP)

Country of Origin: USSR.
Type: General-purpose transport helicopter.
Power Plant: Two 1,500 shp Izotov TB-2-117A turboshafts.
Performance: (At 24,470 lb/11 100 kg) Max. speed, 155 mph (250 km/h); max. cruise, 140 mph (225 km/h); hovering ceiling (in ground effect), 5,900 ft (1 800 m), (out of ground effect), 2,625 ft (800 m); service ceiling, 14,760 ft (4 500 m); range with 6,615 lb (3 000 kg) of freight, 264 mls (425 km).
Weights: Empty (cargo), 15,787 lb (7 171 kg), (passenger), 16,352 lb (7 417 kg); normal take-off, 24,470 lb (11 100 kg); max. take-off (for VTO), 26,455 lb (12 000 kg).
Dimensions: Rotor diam, 69 ft 10¼ in (21,29 m); fuselage length, 59 ft 7⅓ in (18,17 m).
Notes: The Mi-8 has been in continuous production since 1964 for both civil and military tasks. The standard commercial passenger version has a basic flight crew of two or three and 28 four-abreast seats, and the aeromedical version accommodates 12 casualty stretchers and a medical attendant. As a freighter the Mi-8 will carry up to 8,818 lb (4 000 kg) of cargo, and military tasks include assault transport, search and rescue, and anti-submarine warfare. The Mi-8 is now operated by several Warsaw Pact air forces, serving primarily in the support transport role.

MIL MI-12 (HOMER)

Country of Origin: USSR.

Type: Heavy transport helicopter.

Power Plant: Four 6,500 shp Soloviev D-25VF turboshafts.

Performance: Max. speed, 161 mph (260 km/h); cruise, 149 mph (240 km/h); range with max. payload of 78,000 lb (35 380 kg), 310 mls (500 km); service ceiling, 11,500 ft (3 500 m).

Weights: Normal take-off, 213,848 lb (97 000 kg); max. take-off, 231,485 lb (105 000 kg).

Dimensions: Rotor diam (each), 114 ft 9½ in (35,00 m); fuselage length, 121 ft 4 in (37,00 m).

Notes: First flown in the autumn of 1968 and currently the world's largest helicopter, the Mi-12 carries a crew of six of which the pilot, co-pilot, flight engineer and electrician are accommodated on the lower flight deck with the navigator and radio-operator on the upper deck. The Mi-12 employs the dynamic components of the Mi-6 (see page 269), being in effect two Mi-6 power units, main transmissions and main rotors mounted side-by-side at the tips of braced wings, the overall width with the rotors turning being 219 ft 9 in (67,00 m). The Mi-12 was evidently designed to carry loads compatible with those carried by the fixed-wing An-22 transport, and three prototypes have been built. Production was expected to commence during the course of 1971 for both the Soviet Air Forces and *Aeroflot*.

SIAI-MARCHETTI SV-20A

Country of Origin: Italy.

Type: General-purpose transport helicopter.

Power Plant: Two 1,100 shp Pratt & Whitney PT6A-40 turboshafts.

Performance: (Estimated) Max. cruise, 202 mph (324 km/h) at sea level; econ. cruise, 184 mph (296 km/h); hovering ceiling (in ground effect), 23,000 ft (7 010 m), (out of ground effect), 17,500 ft (5 334 m); max. range, 480 mls (890 km).

Weights: Empty, 4,122 lb (1 870 kg); max. take-off, 8,818 lb (4 000 kg).

Dimensions: Rotor diam, 42 ft 2¼ in (12,86 m); fuselage length, 39 ft 3½ in (11,98 m).

Notes: The SV-20A high-speed winged helicopter is scheduled to commence its flight test programme late in 1972, five prototypes being under construction, together with two prototypes of a compound version, the SV-20C. The SV-20C will differ primarily in having a constant-speed pusher airscrew aft of the starboard engine nacelle. Both models will provide accommodation for two crew members and up to 12 passengers, alternative loads including four casualty stretchers and a medical attendant or some 2,750 lb (1 250 kg) of freight. The SV-20C is expected to enter service 1974–75.

SIKORSKY S-58T

Country of Origin: USA.
Type: General-purpose transport helicopter.
Power Plant: One 1,525 shp Pratt & Whitney PT6T-3 coupled turboshaft.
Performance: Max. speed, 123 mph (198 km/h) at sea level; max. cruise, 115 mph (185 km/h); econ. cruise, 92 mph (148 km/h); hovering ceiling (out of ground effect), 6,500 ft (1 980 m); max. range, 480 mls (772 km).
Weights: Empty, 7,300 lb (3 311 kg); max. take-off, 13,000 lb (5 896 kg).
Dimensions: Rotor diam, 56 ft 0 in (17,07 m); fuselage length, 47 ft 3 in (14,4 m).
Notes: The S-58T is a turbine-powered conversion of the piston-engined S-58, affording improved performance, lower operating costs and increased reliability. Design of the S-58T conversion commenced in January 1970, and the prototype conversion was first flown on August 19, 1970. A number of used S-58s have been obtained by Sikorsky Aircraft and are being offered for sale after conversion to turbine power, and the company is also producing retrofit kits to enable S-58 operators to convert their own helicopters to S-58T standards. Some 40 converted helicopters and conversion kits had been delivered by the beginning of 1972. The S-58T has a normal flight crew of two with dual controls, and can accommodate 12–16 passengers.

SIKORSKY S-61A

Country of Origin: USA.
Type: Amphibious transport and rescue helicopter.
Power Plant: (S-61A-4) Two 1,500 shp General Electric T58-GE-5 turboshafts.
Performance: (At 20,500 lb/9 300 kg) Max. speed, 153 mph (248 km/h); range cruise, 126 mph (203 km/h); max. inclined climb, 2,200 ft/min (11,17 m/sec); hovering ceiling (in ground effect), 8,600 ft (2 820 m); range with max. fuel and 10 % reserves, 525 mls (845 km).
Weights: Empty, 9,763 lb (4 428 kg); normal take-off, 20,500 lb (9 300 kg); max., 21,500 lb (9 750 kg).
Dimensions: Rotor diam., 62 ft 0 in (18,90 m); fuselage length, 54 ft 9 in (16,69 m).
Notes: A transport equivalent of the S-61B (see page 283) with sonar, weapons, and automatic blade folding deleted, and a cargo floor inserted, the S-61A is used by the USAF for missile site support as the CH-3B, this having 1,250 shp T58-GE-8Bs and accommodation for 26 troops or 15 stretchers. Eight similarly-powered S-61A-1s supplied to Denmark for the rescue task were supplemented in 1970 by a ninth machine, and 10 T58-GE-5-powered S-61A-4s equipped to carry 31 combat troops and supplied to Malaysia were supplemented during 1971 by six further S-61A-4s. The S-61L and S-61N (see 1967 edition) are non-amphibious and amphibious commercial versions.

SIKORSKY S-61R

Country of Origin: USA.

Type: Amphibious transport and rescue helicopter.

Power Plant: (CH-3E) Two 1,500 shp General Electric T58-GE-5 turboshafts.

Performance: (CH-3E at 21,247 lb/9 635 kg) Max. speed, 162 mph (261 km/h) at sea level; range cruise, 144 mph (232 km/h); max. inclined climb, 1,310 ft/min (6,6 m/sec); hovering ceiling (in ground effect), 4,100 ft (1 250 m); range with 10% reserves, 465 mls (748 km).

Weights: (CH-3E) Empty, 13,255 lb (6 010 kg); normal take-off, 21,247 lb (9 635 kg); max. take-off, 22,050 lb (10 000 kg).

Dimensions: Rotor diam, 62 ft 0 in (18,90 m); fuselage length, 57 ft 3 in (17,45 m).

Notes: Although based on the S-61A, the S-61R embodies numerous design changes, including a rear ramp and a tricycle-type undercarriage. Initial model for the USAF was the CH-3C with 1,300 shp T58-GE-1 turboshafts, but this was subsequently updated to CH-3E standards. The CH-3E can accommodate 25–30 troops or 5,000 lb (2 270 kg) of cargo, and may be fitted with a TAT-102 barbette on each sponson mounting a 7,62-mm Minigun. The HH-3E is a USAF rescue version with armour, self-sealing tanks, and refuelling probe, and the HH-3F Pelican (illustrated) is a US Coast Guard search and rescue model.

SIKORSKY S-62A

Country of Origin: USA.

Type: Amphibious utility transport helicopter.

Power Plant: One 1,250 shp General Electric CT58-110-1 turboshaft.

Performance: Max. speed, 101 mph (163 km/h) at sea level; max. cruise, 92 mph (148 km/h); max. inclined climb, 1,140 ft/min (5,8 m/sec); hovering ceiling (in ground effect), 14,100 ft (4 295 m), (out of ground effect), 4,600 ft (1 400 m); range with 10% reserves, 462 mls (743 km).

Weights: Empty equipped, 4,957 lb (2 248 kg); max. take-off, 7,900 lb (3 583 kg).

Dimensions: Rotor diam, 53 ft 0 in (16,16 m); fuselage length, 44 ft 6½ in (13,58 m).

Notes: The S-62 embodies many components of the piston-engined S-55 (see 1961 edition), including rotor blades and heads, and the basic model is the S-62A which can accommodate 12 troops or 10 airline passengers. The S-62A is licence-built in Japan by Mitsubishi for both military and civil roles, both the Maritime and Air Self-Defence Forces using this type in the rescue role. A US Coast Guard rescue version is designated HH-52A (see 1970 edition), this having a rescue platform, and automatic stabilisation and towing equipment. The HH-52A operates at higher weights, the S-62C being the commercial and military foreign version.

SIKORSKY S-64 SKYCRANE

Country of Origin: USA.
Type: Heavy flying-crane helicopter.
Power Plant: Two 4,500 shp Pratt & Whitney T73-P-1 turboshafts.
Performance: (CH-54A at 38,000 lb/17 237 kg) Max. speed, 127 mph (204 km/h) at sea level; max. cruise, 109 mph (175 km/h); max. inclined climb, 1,700 ft/min (8,64 m/sec); hovering ceiling (in ground effect), 10,600 ft (3 230 m), (out of ground effect), 6,900 ft (2 100 m); range, 253 mls (407 km).
Weights: (CH-54A) Empty, 19,234 lb (8 724 kg); max. take-off, 42,000 lb (19 050 kg).
Dimensions: Rotor diam, 72 ft 0 in (21,95 m); fuselage length, 70 ft 3 in (21,41 m).
Notes: The S-64A serves with the US Army as the CH-54A Tarhe in the heavy lift role, and may be fitted with a 15,000-lb (6 800-kg) hoist or an all-purpose pod (seen fitted above) which can accommodate 45 troops or 24 casualty stretchers. The commercial equivalent of the CH-54A is designated S-64E. A developed version, the CH-54B powered by T73-P-700 turboshafts of 4,800 shp, was flown on June 30, 1969, other changes including dual mainwheels and an increase in max. take-off to 47,000 lb (21 319 kg). The CH-54B also features a new gearbox and high-lift rotor blades, the civil equivalent being the S-64F.

SIKORSKY S-65

Country of Origin: USA.

Type: Heavy assault transport helicopter.

Power Plant: Two 3,925 shp General Electric T64-GE-413 turboshafts.

Performance: Max. speed, 196 mph (315 km/h) at sea level; max. cruise, 173 mph (278 km/h); max. inclined climb, 2,180 ft/min (11,08 m/sec); hovering ceiling (in ground effect), 13,400 ft (4 080 m), (out of ground effect), 6,500 ft (1 980 m); range, 257 mls (413 km).

Weights: Empty, 23,485 lb (10 653 kg); normal take-off, 36,400 lb (16 510 kg); 42,000 lb (19 050 kg).

Dimensions: Rotor diam, 72 ft 3 in (22,02 m); fuselage length, 67 ft 2 in (20,47 m).

Notes: Using many components based on those of the S-64 (see page 277), the S-65 can accommodate 38 combat troops or 24 casualty stretchers and four medical attendants. The initial US Navy version, the CH-53A Sea Stallion, has 2,850 shp T64-GE-6 turboshafts, and the HH-53B for the USAF is similar apart from having 3,080 shp T64-GE-3s, a flight refuelling probe, jettisonable auxiliary tanks and armament, the HH-53C differing primarily in having 3,435 shp T64-GE-7s and an external cargo hook. The US Marine Corps' CH-53D (to which the specification applies) has up-rated engines and can carry up to 64 troops. The CH-53DG for Germany and S-65-Oe for Austria (illustrated) are similar.

278

SIKORSKY S-67 BLACKHAWK

Country of Origin: USA.
Type: Two-seat attack helicopter.
Power Plant: Two 1,500 shp General Electric T58-GE-5 turboshafts.
Performance: (Estimated) Max. speed, 205 mph (330 km/h) at sea level; max. cruise, 195 mph (314 km/h); normal range, 250 mls (402 km).
Weights: Empty, 10,900 lb (4 944 kg); max. take-off (attack configuration), 18,500 lb (8 392 kg); max. overload take-off, 22,000 lb (9 979 kg).
Dimensions: Rotor diam, 62 ft 0 in (18,90 m); fuselage length, 64 ft 4¾ in (19,63 m).
Notes: The S-67 is a company-funded development based on the unsuccessful S-66 entry in the US Army's AAFSS (Advanced Aerial Fire Support System) competition, and rotors, gearboxes, drive shafts, and controls are similar to those of the S-61. As an attack helicopter the S-67 will carry up to 8,000 lb (3 629 kg) of ordnance, including barbette-mounted 7,62-mm Miniguns, 20-mm or 30-mm cannon, or 40-mm grenade launchers, and the 28-ft (8,53-m) fixed wing carries speed brakes to increase combat manoeuvrability. With some cabin modifications the S-67 could transport 15 troops a distance of 220 mls (354 km) at 165 mph (265 km/h), and for the rescue role with auxiliary fuel could fly distances up to 600 mls (966 km).

VFW-FOKKER H3 SPRINTER

Country of Origin: Federal Germany.
Type: Three-seat light compound helicopter.
Power Plant: One 400 hp Allison 250-C20 turboshaft.
Performance: Max. cruise, 155 mph (250 km/h) at sea level; inclined climb, 1,280 ft/min (6,5 m/sec); hovering ceiling (in ground effect), 5,070 ft (1 540 m), (out of ground effect), 1,500 ft (455 m); max. range, 490 mls (790 km).
Weights: Empty, 1,090 lb (495 kg); max. take-off, 2,134 lb (968 kg).
Dimensions: Rotor diam, 28 ft 6½ in (8,70 m); fuselage length, 24 ft 2¼ in (7,37 m).
Notes: The H3 Sprinter was flown for the first time on March 15, 1971, and is intended to be the first in a family of compound helicopters currently planned by VFW-Fokker. The three-blade rotor is tip-driven by compressed air for vertical take-off, hovering and landing, and for transition to forward flight power is progressively transferred to two shrouded seven-bladed airscrews mounted on stub fairings on the fuselage sides. These were not fitted for initial flight trials (as illustrated). In horizontal flight the rotor autorotates, eliminating the need for conventional transmission and drive-shaft systems, hydraulic systems, clutches and torque compensation. In the event of an engine failure full rotor autorotation is maintained.

WESTLAND WASP

Country of Origin: United Kingdom.
Type: Five/six-seat general-purpose and anti-submarine warfare helicopter.
Power Plant: One 710 shp Rolls-Royce Bristol Nimbus 503 turboshaft.
Performance: Max. speed, 120 mph (193 km/h) at sea level; max. cruise, 110 mph (177 km/h); max. inclined climb, 1,440 ft/min (7,4 m/sec); hovering ceiling (in ground effect), 12,500 ft (3 810 m), (out of ground effect), 8,800 ft (2 682 m); max. range with standard fuel, 303 mls (488 km).
Weights: Empty, 3,452 lb (1 566 kg); max. take-off, 5,500 lb (2 495 kg).
Dimensions: Rotor diam, 32 ft 3 in (9,83 m); fuselage length, 30 ft 4 in (9,24 m).
Notes: In its H.A.S. Mk. 1 form, the Wasp serves with the Royal Navy in the anti-submarine weapon-carrying role, operating from platforms aboard frigates equipped with long-range asdic. In this role the Wasp is normally crewed by a single pilot and carries two 270-lb (122,4-kg) torpedoes. Dual controls may be fitted. The Wasp has been supplied to the Brazilian (3), New Zealand (3), Netherlands (12) and South African (10) navies, and consideration was being given to reopening the production line late in 1971 to fulfil a supplementary order from South Africa.

WESTLAND WG.13 LYNX

Country of Origin: United Kingdom.
Type: Multi-purpose and transport helicopter.
Power Plant: Two 900 shp Rolls-Royce BS.360-07-26 turboshafts.
Performance: (Estimated) Max. speed, 184 mph (296 km/h) at sea level; max. cruise, 161 mph (259 km/h); max. inclined climb, 2,500 ft/min (12,7 m/sec); max. range with 10 passengers, 173 mls (278 km), with max. standard fuel and 5% reserves, 495 mls (796 km).
Weights: Empty, 4,920 lb (2 232 kg); empty equipped (average), 5,750 lb (2 812 kg); max. take-off, 8,000 lb (3 620 kg).
Dimensions: Rotor diam, 42 ft 0 in (12,80 m); fuselage length, 40 ft 6 in (12,34 m).
Notes: The Lynx, the first of 12 prototypes of which commenced its flight test programme on March 21, 1971, is one of the three types covered by the Anglo-French helicopter agreement, and production deliveries (to the British Army) are scheduled to commence in the autumn of 1973. To the end of 1980 a total of 277 is programmed for supply to the British armed forces, and current plans call for some 80 examples of an ASW version for France's *Aéronavale* from 1975. The standard Lynx will carry 12 combat troops, up to 2,738 lb (1 242 kg) of freight internally, or a slung load of up to 3,000 lb (1 361 kg).

282

WESTLAND (S-61B) SEA KING

Country of Origin: United Kingdom (US licence).
Type: Amphibious anti-submarine helicopter.
Power Plant: Two 1,500 shp Rolls-Royce Gnome H.1400 turboshafts.
Performance: (At 20,500 lb/9 298 kg) Max. speed, 143 mph (230 km/h); max. cruise, 131 mph (211 km/h); max. endurance cruise, 86 mph (138 km/h); max. inclined climb, 1,770 ft/min (8,97 m/sec); max. range with standard fuel, 690 mls (1 110 km).
Weights: Basic, 12,700 lb (5 760 kg); empty equipped, 15,474 lb (7 019 kg); max. take-off, 21,500 lb (9 751 kg).
Dimensions: Rotor diam, 62 ft 0 in (18,90 m); fuselage length, 54 ft 9 in (16,69 m).
Notes: The Sea King H.A.S. Mk. 1 is an anglicised licence-built version of the Sikorsky S-61B and, apart from equipment, is essentially similar to the US Navy's SH-3D Sea King (see 1968 edition), the Gnome turboshafts being licence-produced derivatives of the General Electric T58. Sixty Westland-built Sea Kings are being delivered to the Royal Navy, 22 have been ordered by Federal Germany, 10 by Norway and six by India. The SH-3A (1,250 shp T58-GE-8B) serves with Canada (CHSS-2) and is licence-built by Mitsubishi, and the SH-3D (1,400 shp T58-GE-10) serves with Italy, Brazil and Spain. The SH-3D is manufactured under licence in Italy by Agusta.

283

ACKNOWLEDGEMENTS

The author wishes to record his thanks to the following sources of copyright photographs appearing in this volume: Blandin-Regnier, page 166; Butler-Green, 24, 120, 136, 272; Roger Demeulle, 166; Howard Levy, 74, 118, 236, 254, 279; Stephen Peltz, 20, 34, 68, 76, 114, 122, 132, 158, 226, 228, 244, 247, 249, 255, 260, 263, 267, 270, 271. The three-view silhouettes are copyright Pilot Press Limited.

INDEX OF AIRCRAFT TYPES

285

Printed for the Publishers by
Butler & Tanner Ltd, Frome and London

Code No. 1944 11.71

Printed for the Publishers by
Butler & Tanner Ltd, Frome and London

Code No. 1944 11.71